I Am Action

I Am Action

Literary and Combat Articles, Thoughts, and Revolutionary Chronicles

Praxedis G. Guerrero

Translated and introduced by
Javier Sethness-Castro

*I Am Action: Literary and Combat Articles, Thoughts, and
Revolutionary Chronicles*

© 2018 Javier Sethness-Castro
This edition © 2018 AK Press (Chico, Edinburgh)

ISBN: 9781849353144
E-ISBN: 9781849353137
Library of Congress Control Number: 2017957074

AK Press	AK Press
370 Ryan Ave. #100	33 Tower St.
Chico, CA 95973	Edinburgh EH6 7BN
United States	Scotland
www.akpress.org	www.akuk.com
akpress@akpress.org	ak@akedin.demon.co.uk

The above addresses would be delighted to provide you with the latest
AK Press distribution catalog, which features books, pamphlets, zines, and
stylish apparel published and/or distributed by AK Press. Alternatively, visit
our websites for the complete catalog, latest news, and secure ordering

Front cover illustration by Alberto Castillo, www.castilloalberto.com
Printed in the USA

TABLE OF CONTENTS

Introduction

The militant Mexican anarchist and revolutionary martyr Praxedis G. Guerrero arguably merits his comrade Ricardo Flores Magón's laudatory characterization of him as a "sublime figure in the revolutionary history of the world."[1] This self-described "warrior, apostle, and philosopher," born in 1882 to an aristocratic family in the highlands of Guanajuato State, was "destined to be one of the principal precursors" of the Mexican Revolution, according to his biographer Ward S. Albro.[2] During his short but highly illuminating life, Guerrero participated as a central figure in the transnational revolutionary network established by the Organizational Council of the Mexican Liberal Party (PLM), which was dedicated firstly to deposing the tyrant Porfirio Díaz and thereafter to promoting anarchist revolution throughout Mexico according to the slogan *Tierra y Libertad* ("Land and Freedom").

As Magón writes in his reminisces about Guerrero following his death early in the Revolution, there was little immediate indication from the childhood of Praxedis, whose father was a local indigenous chief and whose mother was the daughter of a Spanish count, that he would be anything other than bourgeois. His family's hacienda in Los Altos de Ibarra, Guanajuato, comprised thousands of acres that were worked by hundreds of farmhands.

---

1   See "A Letter from Ricardo Flores Magón" in this volume.

2   Ward S. Albro, *To Die on Your Feet: The Life, Times, and Writings of Praxedis G. Guerrero* (Fort Worth: Texas Christian University, 1996), 2.

Yet Praxedis was privileged to have developed an "exceptional sensitivity" and an "exceptional brain" that led him to adopt the revolutionary proletarian cause upon his maturation.[3] At eighteen, he left with his brother for San Luis Potosí, where they worked for a number of months in a brewery and smelter. Thereafter he returned to Guanajuato to work in the family business for some time before enlisting in the Second Military Reserve under General Bernardo Reyes, Díaz's minister of war and appointed governor of Nuevo León State. Rising to the rank of Second Lieutenant of cavalry, Praxedis received the military training that would later serve the PLM's cause. He resigned his post after the 2 April 1902 massacre in Monterrey ordered by Reyes against Liberal protesters who were mobilizing in favor of another gubernatorial candidate. Around the same time, Guerrero became acquainted with Mexico's Liberal oppositional press, including the satirical newspaper *El Hijo del Ahuizote* ("The Son of the Ahuizote"),[4] edited by Juan Sarabia from August 1885 until July 1902, when Ricardo and Enrique Flores Magón rented out the press, and presumably *Regeneración* ("Regeneration"), founded by Jesús and Ricardo Flores Magón in August 1900.[5] After resigning his military post, he returned to Guanajuato to attend to his ill father and manage the family's *hacienda*, and it was from his father's bookshelf that Praxedis first encountered the writings of Victor Hugo, Maxim Gorky, Lev Tolstoy, Mikhail Bakunin, and Peter Kropotkin.

In 1904, consummating the dream Tolstoy had envisioned but could never effect, Guerrero definitively abandoned his aristocratic

3   See "A Letter from Ricardo Flores Magón."

4   The ahuizote (from the Nahuatl *ahuitzotl*, "spiky aquatic thing") is a creature from Aztec legend that likely refers to the axolotl (*Ambystoma mexicanum*), an amphibian species that characteristically does not metamorphose upon maturation.

5   Diego Abad de Santillán, *Ricardo Flores Magón: El apóstol de la Revolución mexicana* (México, D.F.: Editorial RedeZ, "Tejiendo la Utopía," 2011), 26; Claudio Lomnitz, *The Return of Comrade Ricardo Flores Magón* (New York: Zone Books, 2014), 83.

upbringing. With his comrades Francisco Manrique and Manuel Vázquez, he left Mexico for the U.S., where he sold his labor as a miner in Colorado, a lumberjack in Texas, a longshoreman in San Francisco, and a copper and coal miner in Arizona. He founded the newspaper *Alba Roja* ("Red Dawn") with Francisco and Manuel while in San Francisco, and it was likely in this way that he brought himself to the attention to the newly established Organizational Council of the Mexican Liberal Party, founded in St. Louis in 1905 by the exiled radicals Ricardo and Enrique Flores Magón, Juan and Manuel Sarabia, Librado Rivera, Antonio I. Villarreal, and Rosalío Bustamante. In Douglas, Arizona, Praxedis met and befriended Manuel Sarabia and requested successfully to affiliate himself with the PLM. Days after the suppression of the June 1906 Cananea strike in the desert of Sonora, which had been launched by thousands of Mexican miners demanding an eight-hour work day and higher wages, Praxedis founded the organization "Free Workers" with his comrades toward the end of propagating the Liberal ideal among the miners of the region. He also established a local PLM group in Morenci counting some fifty members, as a counterpart to the Liberal Club of Douglas. The failure of the Council's plans for an insurrection against the dictatorship in the border towns of Ciudad Juárez, Nogales, and Jiménez—a plot that was organized to coincide with Independence Day, 16 September 1906—and the subsequent arrest of Ricardo, Antonio, and Librado in Los Angeles for having violated existing neutrality laws between the U.S. and Mexico launched Guerrero into the position of principal responsibility for the cause. Indeed, as Albro argues, Praxedis effectively led the PLM's struggle during the three highly significant years of 1907 to 1910, corresponding to the time that the Council's better-known organizers were imprisoned, and ending with his death in the Revolution.[6]

Praxedis was named a "Special Delegate" of the PLM's Organizational Council in June 1907, and the next month he distributed a public call for justice in the case of Manuel Sarabia, his comrade

6   Albro, 138.

and roommate in Douglas, Arizona, who had been kidnapped, deported, and imprisoned in Hermosillo, Sonora, at the hands of Díaz's henchmen. This crime sparked an international outcry that resulted in Sarabia's release following a show trial that acquitted the militant's captors. Then, following the arrest of another exiled Liberal, Lázaro Gutiérrez de Lara, Guerrero moved to Los Angeles to collaborate with Sarabia and Enrique Flores Magón in editing and publishing the newspaper *Revolución*, which began its run in June 1907. Sarabia was soon arrested on the very same charges as Magón, Villarreal, and Rivera, but was subsequently rescued by Elizabeth Trowbridge, a socialist activist and heiress from Boston, who paid his bail, married him, and escaped with to England. Although Praxedis cut off communication with Manuel over this decision to elope, Sarabia nonetheless would circulate Guerrero's writings throughout much of the European continent.[7] Praxedis had his first meeting with Ricardo, Antonio, and Librado in the Los Angeles jail in November 1907; the next month, he was named Second Secretary of the Organizational Council. *Revolución* was subsequently shut down, its press destroyed and its editors incarcerated by L.A. police acting on behalf of the Mexican State. Whereas Praxedis and Enrique saw the light of day thanks to the efforts of some comrades, their co-editor Modesto Díaz died in prison.[8]

Seeking to relaunch the Revolution against Díaz, Praxedis left Los Angeles with Francisco Manrique for El Paso, where they organized a widespread insurrection in Mexico, set for 24–25 June 1908. Guerrero commanded some sixty armed Liberal groups divided across five geographical zones comprising Mexico that were prepared to revolt.[9] Nonetheless, as in the case of the uprising organized two years prior, this new revolutionary plan was largely

---

7   Ibid., 112.

8   Ibid, 35–37.

9   Benjamin Maldonado, "Biographical Sketch" in *Dreams of Freedom: A Ricardo Flores Magón Reader*, eds. Chaz Bufe and Mitchell Cowen Verter (Oakland: AK Press, 2005), 83.

foiled by the two States' transnational spy network: hundreds of conspirators were arrested and sent to the San Juan de Ulúa prison in Veracruz, where many perished. Still, Liberal forces managed to engage in three battles against federal troops during this time: in Las Vacas, Coahuila, a village which the Liberals likely would have taken, had they not run out of ammunition during the firefight; Viesca, Coahuila, where the insurgents liberated the local jail, expropriated State funds, and proclaimed the PLM's program, but were driven out by Díaz's forces; and Palomas, Chihuahua, an attack that Praxedis personally led, but which led to the death of his comrade Francisco. Guerrero commemorates these three revolutionary episodes in heroic chronicles translated in this volume. The pathos permeating the "Palomas" chronicle celebrates Francisco's martyrdom, serving both to foreshadow Guerrero's own end and to laud the revolutionary commitment of his childhood friend, who, like Praxedis, had been born into wealth but who had repudiated such privilege to dedicate himself wholeheartedly to the struggle.

Despite the failures of the 1908 uprisings, Guerrero continued organizing the Revolution unfazed. In early 1909, he traveled to central and southern Mexico on a mission authorized by the Council to coordinate a new simultaneous uprising on both sides of the border. During this trip, he also visited his family in Guanajuato for the last time, announcing to them that he had become a vegetarian because "it hurt him that animals were sacrificed" and that he renounced the inheritance left to him by his late father for being inconsistent with anarchism.[10] Upon return to the U.S., he undertook a tour of the Midwest to request support from the Socialist Party for the coming Revolution. By this time, U.S. and Mexican authorities had come to realize the threat posed by Guerrero, with the Mexican consul referring to him as the *"revoltoso chief"* and the Secretary of State identifying him as a "notorious

10 Eugenio Martínez Núñez, *La vida heroica de Práxedis G. Guerrero* (México: Instituto Nacional de Estudios Históricos de la Revolución, 1960), 51.

revolutionist who is still at large."[11] In fact, in Houston in early 1910, the militant narrowly escaped capture at the hands of a U.S. marshal by reportedly climbing out a third-story hotel window.

Thereafter, in El Paso, Praxedis founded *Punto Rojo* ("Flash Point") as a successor to *Revolución*, and this periodical enjoyed an estimated weekly circulation of ten-thousand copies, primarily among Mexican laborers in the U.S. Southwest. Guerrero also founded the Pan-American Labor League in San Antonio in the summer of 1910. Once Ricardo, Antonio, and Librado were released from prison in August 1910, Praxedis left Texas for Los Angeles, where the Organizational Council was reconstituted and *Regeneración* relaunched. Guerrero had dozens of his most important articles published in this newspaper during the three months he spent with his comrades before his final departure, and several more were published in its pages posthumously.

Upon the proclamation of the Mexican Revolution in November 1910, as issued by Magón's reformist rival Francisco I. Madero, Liberal combat-units were activated throughout much of the country: in Sonora, Chihuahua, Tlaxcala, Morelos, Durango, Oaxaca, Tabasco, and Veracruz. Believing that his aloofness from the battlefield contradicted his anarchist principles, Praxedis departed Los Angeles for El Paso to join the Revolution, much to the consternation of Magón and other comrades on the Council. Leading a group of insurgents who flew the red flag emblazoned with the slogan *Tierra y Libertad* across the border into Mexico on December 19, Guerrero had planned to liberate a number of communities in Chihuahua before marching on the state's capital city.

After having attacked the Cruz González *hacienda* and taking the train south to Guzmán station, destroying bridges along the way, the rebels divided into two groups, with the column commanded by Praxedis attempting first to take Casas Grandes. Such a task appeared impossible due to the vast discrepancy in forces between the Liberals and federal troops, so the insurgents retreated northwest to the town of Janos, which they took on December 30

11 Albro 55–59.

after fierce fighting. Nevertheless, federal reinforcements arrived shortly after this victory, and it was during this battle that Guerrero and some eleven other militants lost their lives. Greatly moved by the deaths of their comrades, the Liberal troops repelled the reinforcements, though they ultimately had to withdraw and leave the bodies of Guerrero and the others behind. Thus ended the life of Praxedis, the revolutionary anarcho-communist whose existence "had given off such intense light."[12]

***

Though his position as commander of the multitude of PLM armed units and his tragic death on the battlefield of the Mexican Revolution may give one the impression that Praxedis was first and foremost a guerrilla fighter, he instead understood his primary obligation as a revolutionary to agitate through his writings. This "free man, of a prodigious intelligence, of indomitable courage, blessed with an astonishing energy and with love for the people, without limits or duplicity," as described by Isidoro Lois in the Cuban anarchist newspaper *¡Tierra!*, closely mirrors the example of his comrade Magón.[13] He is also reminiscent of his teacher Kropotkin, whose volumes he was often seen carrying around, leading those close to him to call him the "apostle of Kropotkin."[14] Indeed, in the article "Laboring" (1910), Praxedis defines the task of the revolutionary as "ignit[ing] with the fire of his [or her] word the extinguished consciences, sowing rebelliousness and discontent." This task, which the militant often accomplishes using naturalistic imagery and extended metaphor, was one to which Praxedis

12 Ricardo Flores Magón, "Praxedis G. Guerrero," in this volume.

13 Jacinto Barrera and Alejandro de la Torre, eds, *Los rebeldes de la bandera roja: Textos del periódico anarquista* ¡Tierra!, *de La Habana, sobre la Revolución mexicana* (Mexico City: Instituto Nacional de Antropología e Historia, 2011), 215.

14 Albro, 104.

dedicated himself for the last decade of his life, from adolescence to the Mexican Revolution.

The present volume includes the translation of forty articles by Guerrero and five entries by Magón, including two of the latter's short stories, doubtlessly written with the revolutionary martyr in mind. The work is a translation of Praxedis's collected writings as published in 1924 by the Grupo Cultural Ricardo Flores Magón, being comprised of Nicolás Bernal, Librado Rivera, and Diego Abad de Santillán. These combative-journalistic writings demonstrate the faithful observation Praxedis made of the revolutionary task he set for himself and others, illustrating his passionate championing of the cause of the oppressed against the three-headed hydra of Capital, Authority, and the Clergy. They serve as a testament to the optimism and commitment of one of the central figures of the PLM's Organizational Council who, together with the Magón brothers and Rivera, advanced a redemptory anarcho-communist vision that contrasted with the gradualist opportunism evinced by Antonio Villarreal and Juan and Manuel Sarabia, who would side with Maderismo early on in the Revolution. Dialectically, though, the split between incrementalists and radicals in the PLM would finally allow the Council openly to proclaim its anarchism, as it would do in the Manifesto it issued nearly a year after Praxedis's death, thus overturning the more reformist Program it had first published in 1906.

Yet, however revolutionary were and are Guerrero's life and writings, the conscious contemporary reader may find some of his formulations rather disconcerting. For one, though he identified as an anarchist, racism is hardly overthrown in his essays, considering the problematic association he makes between Africans and barbarism in an essay denouncing a white-supremacist gang for burning a Mexican youth alive in Texas ("Whites, Whites," 1910). In point of fact, seemingly greatly taken with the progressivist-rationalist aspects of anarchism, Praxedis expresses Eurocentric perspectives, given his view of various cultural aspects of pre-Hispanic Mexican society as being barbarous: for example, human sacrifice to Huitzilopochtli, "the worship of lizards," and body piercings

("Women," 1910). In keeping with this—perhaps retaining pride in his half-Spanish heritage—Guerrero repeatedly cites Columbus in a positive light! He was surely no indigenist.

Furthermore, though he defended the cause of women's emancipation—stipulating this as one of the "grand principles" of the "Program of the Pan-American Labor League" (1910), and dedicating a few articles to women's struggles—he expresses his opposition to mainstream contemporary feminism, vehemently upholds the gender binary, and at times portrays women in sexist ways. What is more, his writings on sexuality are traditionalist and heterosexist, as they seemingly favor monogamy and explicitly condemn homosexuality—this, despite the rather homoerotic descriptions Praxedis would pen of his martyred Liberal comrades in the revolutionary chronicles detailing the summer 1908 uprisings, especially Francisco Manrique.

This chronological translation of Guerrero's writings goes to press under the Trump regime, which represents a regurgitation of Díaz from the past—and, as in Mexico a century before, a despotism that only revolution would be able to end justly. In this sense, it is significant for present-day struggles that the last two essays Praxedis had published while alive address some of the various customs and practices that uphold patriarchy on the global stage and the previously mentioned murder by incineration of a Mexican migrant worker at the hands of Anglo proto-fascists: "Women" and "Whites, Whites." Guerrero's commitment to social transformation across borders and the militant's emphasis on direct action undoubtedly retain all their relevance today.

—Javier Sethness-Castro

Translator's Note

This translation is based primarily on Praxedis Guerrero's *Artículos literarios y de combate; pensamientos; crónicas revolucionarias, etc.* published by the Grupo Cultural Ricardo Flores Magón in 1924. That volume is also the source of the letter and articles included here that were written by Magón after Guerrero's death, as well as of the version of Guerrero's "Flash Points" that is translated here. Please note that these do not include all of the "Flash Points," but rather those chosen by the original volume's editors: Nicolás Bernal, Librado Rivera, and Diego Abad de Santillán. I have complemented the 1924 volume with the more complete version *Artículos de Combate*, published by Editorial RedeZ, "Tejiendo la Utopía" in 2013. All of Guerrero's writings translated here were originally published in the periodicals *Revolución*, *Punto Rojo*, or *Regeneración*, and are indicated as such. The pieces from the latter publication date from *Regeneración*'s fourth edition, which began in September 1910 and ended in March 1918. The two short stories by Magón included here, which feature protagonists strongly suggestive of Guerrero, appear in *Obra Literaria: Cuentos. Relatos. Teatro*, by Ricardo Flores Magón, edited by Jacinto Barrera Bassols (Mexico City: Consejo Nacional Para La Cultura y Las Artes, 2009). When one considers that the first of these stories ("The Apostle") came out in the issue of *Regeneración* published a week after Praxedis's martyrdom, and that the second ("A Catastrophe") appears in the periodical a year and two weeks after the youth's premature death, it becomes clear that Magón meant "the Delegate" and "Juan," respectively, to represent Guerrero.

All footnotes are mine unless otherwise indicated. I wish to kindly thank Claudio Lomnitz; my mother, María Castro; and Charles Weigl for their help improving the translation.

I Am Action is dedicated to all Mexican, Syrian, and Palestinian revolutionaries: past, present, and future.

I.
Literary and Combat Articles

Justice!

The voice of the people has risen, angry and righteous; popular action drives the authors of the kidnapping of Manuel Sarabia to the dock of the accused.[1] They are all there: the drunk rogue Maza, the police officers who sold the vileness of their consciences, and the despicable chauffer who set a record for criminal complicity. Not even the chief of the Cossack bandits is missing; nor is this other bench empty, for it is occupied by the ferocious supreme judge who ordered the crime and who paid the mercenary hands that strangled Sarabia and wrung out the American flag. The tribunal is forming; the proceedings begin. Let us cross-examine one of the suspects.

Antonio Maza, a man with base instincts, drunk, sycophantic, cowardly, and servile—a professional thug—was the director of the abominable attack.[2] He used trickery, corruption, and infamy to take advantage of an innocent man. He worked, according to his testimony, out of love for the Tsar and under the belief that the Consul would assure him impunity for trampling universal justice and mocking an entire nation.[3]

1 This article denouncing the July 1907 kidnapping of *Regeneración* editor Manuel Sarabia was distributed broadly among the populace of Douglas, Arizona.

2 Antonio Maza (1872–?), Mexican vice-consul in Douglas, AZ.

3 The allusion to the Tsar is a reference to Porfirio Díaz, given that he was often likened by Mexican radicals and their supporters to the Russian Emperor.

The ruffians, who sold their dignity for a few coins and covered the star-spangled banner with a heretic's sackcloth, handed over the victim to his tormentors.[4] In their defense they allege complete ignorance of honor and patriotism. Savages would be ashamed to have them as compatriots.

The chauffer: this man had no scruples and, like the others, a rather elastic conscience that was at the disposal of the highest bidder; he was offered a generous tip and worked wonders to earn it. For half a dozen dollars, he would have helped rob half of humanity.

The Cossack colonel, the praetorian Kosterlizky, obeyed superior orders: being the loyal attack dog of the dictator Díaz, his task is to bite the Tsar's enemies.[5] He does not think about the iniquity of the act; the pleasure he takes in exercising his savage Tatar instincts against the defenseless populace suffices.

Let us consider the other, the one with white hair and the look of a decrepit feline: that bloody Maztla, who stirs in his lair of impure senility, terrorizing, ordering crime after crime, rape after rape, and one execution by firing-squad after another. The shadow of the rights he has murdered haunt and pursue him; sometimes this specter takes the form of a woman, while at other times it is a child or an elder, and Abdul, shaken by remorse and fear, orders his janissaries to carry out another massacre.[6] Feverish and ferocious, Tiberius arises, galvanized by ignoble ambition upon hearing the sigh of freedom from this side of the Bravo River, exclaiming, "Who dares to call herself free while I live?"[7] But let's not narrate

4   This sackcloth (*sanbenito*) was a garment worn by heretics condemned in the Spanish Inquisition.

5   Emilio Kosterlizky (1853–1928), the Mexican general who arrested and imprisoned Manuel Sarabia upon receiving him from his US captors.

6   A reference either to the Ottoman sultan Abdul Hamid I (1725–1789) or Abdul Hamid II (1842–1918). Janissaries are elite Turkish infantry.

7   Tiberius Claudius Nero (42 BCE–37 CE), the second Emperor of the Roman Empire.

his life; let's not make a funereal procession of the legion of martyrs sacrificed by this dwarfish brother of Timurlane and Christian II, this accomplice of Ludovico the Moor and Estrada Cabrera. [8]

We speak of a single act: the scandalous assault committed against the defenseless dignified Mexican, Manuel Sarabia.

Porfirio Díaz was the hand that moved all the threads of the drama. Not satisfied with having caught the Mexican nation in the trap of Tuxtepec, not content with having robbed even the shirt from a wretched people, he wants more. After stabbing popular suffrage in the back and slaying the Constitution, after filling the prisons with citizens and causing free thought to die in slavery, as he was admiring the corpse of freedom hanging from an *ahuehuete* in Chapultepec, he devised yet another injustice. [9] He told himself: the work of pacification isn't complete; my spit must reach Capitol Hill and the boots of my thugs must splatter the land of

8   Timurlane, also known as Timur (1336–1405 CE), was a Turkic-Mongol military leader who attempted to restore Genghis Khan's Empire. Praxedis presumably refers also to Christian II of Denmark (1481–1559 CE), known as "Christian the Tyrant," among the Swedes, who infamously slaughtered much of the Swedish nobility after conquering the country. As Regent of Milan, Ludovico Maria Sforza, known as "the Moor" (1452–1508), entered into an alliance with the French Charles VIII to counterbalance the coalition forged between Naples and Rome, leading to the French occupation of both Naples and Milan. The Guatemalan President Manuel José Estrada Cabrera (1857–1924) notoriously granted vast concessions to the United Fruit Company and engaged in repressive strike-breaking.

9   "Tuxtepec" refers to the Tuxtepec Revolution of 1878—first announced in the eponymous Oaxacan city in 1876—whereby Díaz seized power from the Liberal President Sebastián Lerdo de Tejada. *Ahuehuete* is a tree (*Taxodium mucronatum*), otherwise known as Montezuma cypress, while Chapultepec alludes to the forested region of Mexico City (meaning "hill of grasshoppers" in Nahuatl) that served as a retreat for Aztec rulers and later as the site of residence for the colonial rulers of Mexico, a function it still serves.

Lincoln with mud, so that those Mexican rebels who don't live under my whip will die like dogs. And nothing stopped him from carrying out his sinister projects; he did not retreat before Jefferson's frown. He pampered his lackeys with the prospect of abject honors; he encouraged his brutal agents, scattered the gold stolen from the people, and cynically entered the honor of the American people as an item in his accounting book. But... senseless man! Believing himself wrapped in shadow, he did not see that an irritated and angry eye was watching him. Surrounded by buffoons, he thought that the atmosphere of servility and adulation around him extended throughout the American continent. Fool! At this moment, Human Right, the guardian and defender of the weak, has caught him by the throat like a vulgar criminal and has dragged him before the final tribunal of public opinion.

The punishment of the perpetrators begins now; some will be subjected to the law, while others, perhaps the more responsible ones—those who carry decorations on their uniforms and the red-hot mark of universal disdain on their foreheads—nervously await the cry of Spartacus; they see appear the threatening silhouette of the gallows built by the serfs.

Wielding the whip of its virile civic sense, the American people have lashed the nation-killer Porfirio Díaz in the face, which pales not from shame but from fear. The Mexican people must cleanse the Porfirian stain from their country's name. To us—flagellated, humiliated, sold-out, and outlaws in our own country—falls the vindication of our honor! We are lost if fear restrains us! Eternal curses on the coward, on those whose lack of patriotism disowns our glorious past! Let us erase the word tyranny from the country's soil and replace it with another word, on which rests the only peace acceptable for humanity: JUSTICE!

Revolución no. 9, 27 July 1907

Make Way!

From the cluster of clouds that the hurricane swirls around, darkening the sky, emerges the flaming sword wielded by an invisible arm that writes with dazzling zigzags on the roaring page of black smoke the words "MAKE WAY!"[1] The denser is the shadow, the greater that sword's brilliance shines.

From the storm of hatred that surrounds us, from the black bosom of the tempests that tyranny unleashes over our heads, come the invulnerable sword of the Idea, writing with the lightning of the word, in that very heart of darkness, pages honoring the inextinguishable cry of "MAKE WAY!"

We climb without faltering toward the summit; we encounter obstacles, but the rocks do not detain us. If we come across chasms that cut off our path, we cast over them, as if they were a bridge, the words "MAKE WAY!"—and we cross. Amidst the sinister jungle of daggers, we push aside the undergrowth and jump from field to workshop, from dungeon to tomb, from school to barracks, all the while scourging traitors and spies; we advance saying, "MAKE WAY!"

1   As a demonstration of our complete impartiality and solely with the healthy purpose of telling about the rapid evolutionary process suffered by the privileged brain of that profound thinker, Praxedis G. Guerrero, we reproduce this beautiful literary article, "Make Way!," which was published by that great warrior in *Revolución* (Los Angeles, California) in 1907, two years before he wrote the beautiful articles and thoughts published in *Punto Rojo* and *Regeneración* [Bernal, Rivera, and Santillán].

Our progress does not stop to contemplate the crude walls that oppress our brothers: their indomitable spirit has broken the locks and passed beyond the security forces.[2] It has scornfully told the sentinels, "MAKE WAY!" and it has joined us on the path to the future.

Chimerical men, hurled by criminal decadence to the summit of power—dullards, sleepwalkers—do you not feel the gestation of fire? The mountain will launch you into the abyss when it explodes, roaring, "MAKE WAY!"

From the depths of the ancient chest that holds the historically cherished relics, one has been removed. Beautiful, delicate hands will encircle the guerrilla's chest with it: the red shirt, terror of all banners, which tells the Praetorians: "MAKE WAY!"

The old saber of Ayutla and the *Reforma* explodes angrily from the rusty scabbard—"MAKE WAY" for the heroic weapons of the redeeming struggles![3]

We arrive with serene hearts at the door of glorious death and we knock with hilts of steel, crying, "MAKE WAY!"

Revolución no. **14, 14 September 1907**

---

2   A reference to the contemporary imprisonment of Ricardo Flores Magón, Librado Rivera, and Alejandro Villarreal in Arizona for having participated in the 1906 insurrection against Díaz.

3   An allusion to the Plan of Ayutla (1854) declared against the dictatorial General Santa Anna and the Liberal Reform period that followed, producing the Constitution of 1857 From *Ayotlan*, Nahuatl for "near the place of many turtles."

Listen

Do you hear? It is the wind that sways the fronds of the mysterious jungle! The breeze of the future that awakens the still and sleepy undergrowth: it is the first sigh of the virgin rainforest after receiving the kiss of the impetuous Aeolus upon her bowed head.[1]

Do you hear? It is the wind that rips an invisible mantle from the recesses of the sleeping mountain, the wind of an idea that blows through the branches of the immense people, the forest of souls; it is the initial gust that shakes the oak trees, the open face of the hurricane that sweeps, from depths and summit, the confused mist of sterile resignation.

A gentle and fecund breath traverses the jungle; each leaf that it touches is a voice that is born, each branch that moves is an arm being armed: a voice that joins the heroic concert that salutes the redeeming future, the arm that reaches to find the breast of a tyrant.

This is the breath of the Revolution.

Do you feel it? It is the tremble of cracking granite, beaten by the iron fists of Pluto;[2] it is the heart of the world beating within an enormous chest; it is the igneous spirit of a giant shattering his prison to launch his fiery word into space.

It is the earthquake that announces the birth of a volcano.

Do you feel it? Those are the vibrations of divine hammers pounding in the depths of the abyss. It is the life that sprouts from

1   The Greek god of wind.
2   Pluto, otherwise known as Hades, the Greek god governing the underworld.

the black vortex, shaking death's asylum, where dismal vampires reign.

It is the thrust of the advancing Revolution.

Revolución no. 21, 9 November 1907

Fighters, Let's Get to Work!

We force our way through and multiply our action. As long as the nation is enslaved, we should not take a single hour of rest. As long as prison deprives our fallen brothers of movement and light, it is criminal to shackle our feet with indolence. Let us advance; the path lies before us, awaiting. The removal of the warriors surprised by betrayal shows us the dangers at hand, not so that we avoid them but rather so that, in defeating them, we overcome them.[1]

We cannot pause for a moment because the cry of our comrades—traitorously imprisoned heroes—calls us to fulfill our duty. We cannot sleep because our conscience keeps vigil in the night of misfortune, showing us the bloodied body of the nation, abandoned to the teeth of the jackal, the curved beak of the vulture, the ferocious fury of the executioner. Our eyes, always open, cannot turn away from this Dante-esque vision, nestled in shadow. Let us enlarge the flame of our torch by blowing on it with all the force of our lungs until it dispels the horrific scene with its red resplendence.

The wounds of the mother country are infected; let us take up the red-hot ember and apply it to them without delay. The fire chases the beasts away; let us add fuel to our bonfire, and its radiance will grow. By overwhelming the tiger's oblique pupil, we will strengthen the cause.

1   "Betrayal" is a reference to Praxedis's imprisoned comrades from the PLM's Organizational Council. See footnote 2 in "Make Way!" above.

Let us not waste a minute. Let us not squander even a second at leisure. Let us give our nerves the rapid vibration of an electric current to shock the atmosphere out of the dreadful quietism that suffocates our land. The scourge of tyranny falls implacably on our martyred brothers; its continuous crack is a shameful whistle that reaches our ears, that rings provocative and bloody above our heads, wounding our indomitable souls and exciting the tempest of our hatreds.

Fighters, let's get to work! Our task is to struggle without pause. We will not let the number of sacrificed burgeon without reducing the number of those who sacrifice others. Let us unleash the blows of our fists and untie the torment within our minds. If we cannot advance toward freedom by walking, let us jump. Let us expend our energy without fearing exhaustion. Patriotism and will have an endless flow of power. To delay our march and to stay behind those who fall without rushing forward to avenge them, to remain silent, to catch our breath instead of taking up the sword and storming into the breach to crush the enemy is to desert the glorious vanguard. Let us double our efforts. We can rest when the body of the old buffoon of Tuxtepec, hanging at the end of a rope, serves as a plumb bob for the architect of the Future to raise the walls of the people's house.[2]

Revolución no. 21, 9 November 1907

---

2   Tuxtepec, Oaxaca, where Díaz announced his insurgency against the Liberals in 1876. See footnote 9 in "Justice!" above.

Boxer

The tough fight we have kept up has not weakened our forces; the rebellions of our souls continue to hurl the accusatory lightning bolt at the heads of the wicked ones. We have been on the edge of an abyss, the hatred of the powerful, and we have stepped forward without a tremor in our hearts because we know that the heights become a summit when they are approached by the truth.

Many of our comrades have fallen, and a threat hangs over us; a starving pack of hounds besieges us, waiting for the moment to sink its fangs in. Today, tomorrow, at any hour, in whatever place, we might succumb; but in the meantime our pen, a tireless and destructive claw, continues inexorably and tenaciously to storm the trenches of crime, opening the path to a vengeful and just future, because the vengeance of the people is the justice of human rights, when these are judged against the privileges of the master.

Our silence will only come with death. But still, the rebellious pen that we clutch will keep relentlessly slitting Caesar's cloak to show the sword the path to his rotten heart. The immortal spirit of the Revolution that identifies with this sword will find a hundred hands ready to succeed us in the struggle. The tyrants may very well eliminate us as well as our comrades, but they would not advance even an inch by doing so. They will only succeed in making the bonfire of rebellion even bigger. They will only more quickly have to face the ultimate collar: the noose.

Our battle is epic; we have our chains as weapons, which we will break over the heads of despots. We will not cover our breasts: naked as they are, we offer them to the shots of the henchmen. We have laid out the dilemma in this way—life or death: life for us is triumph, and death is the only force that can block our path.

We stand upright, and will never kneel to any power. We will face the enemy; we will not turn our back to any danger.

Revolución no. 26, 14 December 1907

Vile Hatreds

The waves of the sea become choppy in order to kiss the clouds; the Furies of the wicked bubble spit onto what is above their baseness.

The conscience of despots, a dirty pool, can only mimic the ocean's turbulence.

The deep and bitter waves of the ocean's liquid abyss open an immense tomb for men and ships, their rickety toys. The turbid mire of the tyrants' vile souls tries to turn its bosom into a narrow grave for that which is as great as infinity, free thought, the rebellious word, truth, justice, and liberty—but the stingy, the contemptible, and the awful will never have the magnitude of multitudes.

The boiling swamp will not usurp the whirlwind's frenzy.

The miasma that poisons will never be the cloud that incubates lightning.

Though Díaz and his brothers-in-crime feel infernal fury, they will always be ponds that can only produce bubbles.

Though snakes may scale mountains, they still have to crawl to reach those they hope to bite.

At the heights of their all-embracing power, Díaz and his accomplices never stood higher than the rest of the reptiles. Never will they, like an eagle, fall upon the enemy from above: they'll always be hidden in the thicket, waiting for a bare foot to bite— spying on their victims' dreams in order to strangle them. Vile hatreds ferment in their wicked breasts.

Vile hatreds engage us in combat.

We are not in the lair of the tiger, but rather in the rattlesnake's nest. To fight against tigers would be beautiful; to crush snakes is revolting.

The swamp's vapors want to reach our lungs. The circling birds of prey dream of our throats.

Vile hatreds glide by our door.

Revolución no. 29, 25 January 1908

Passivity and Rebellion

In the damp corners of miserable dwellings are produced dark, vis-
cous beings, often clumsy, who also engage in the struggle for life,
exploiting the environment that produces them—the infected, nox-
ious, unwholesome mire—without which their existence would not
provoke the disgust of beings who grew in different environments.

It is possible that the bug comes to believe itself, in good faith,
the protector and savior of the black, humid corner and that it
endeavors to prevent the sun and the broom from entering, rev-
olutionizing, and transforming the medium by destroying it and
its products. Doing so fulfills its duty of self-preservation, because
where would it go without miasmas, darkness, and putrefaction?

Passivity writhes in resistance to the progressive impulse of
revolution.

The myriapoda[1] and the arachnids, the scorpions and burying
beetles—the world of vermin living off the poverty of the people—
practice postures and skillful slitherings to dodge and delay the
blow of the broom and the rays of the sun.

They defend their environment of conventionalism and ener-
vation, because it guarantees their vitality to the constant detriment of the mass of producers.

The quiescent ones raise an outcry calling themselves apostles
of evolution, condemning everything that has any hint of rebelliousness; they appeal to fear and make pathetic patriotic calls;

---

1   A subphylum of arthropods that includes centipedes and
millipedes.

they resort to ignorance and go so far as to advise the people to let themselves be murdered and insulted during the next round of elections, to again and again peacefully exercise their right to vote, so that the tyrants mock them and assassinate them over and over. No mention of leaving the fetid corner, which they propose to improve by adding more and more filth, more and more cowardice.

A somersault within a cubic centimeter of slime, they say, represents a salvational evolution, a peaceful and necessary evolution—necessary, that is, to those who are in their element, in the medium that creates and nurtures them—but not for those of us who seek a pure, clean, and healthy environment, one that only the Revolution can create by destroying the existing despots as well as, very essentially, the socio-economic conditions that have produced them and that would cause new ones to sprout, if we were foolish enough to only end the effects and to allow the causes to remain—that is, if we were to evolve as do they, the inert ones, taking a dive in their cubic centimeter of mud.

True evolution that will improve of the lives of Mexicans, rather than their parasites, will come with the Revolution. The two complement each other, and the former cannot coexist with the anachronisms and subterfuges that the redeemers of passivity employ today.

To evolve we must be free, and we cannot have freedom if we are not rebels, because no tyrant whatsoever has respected passive people. Never has a flock of sheep instilled the majesty of its harmless number upon the wolf that craftily devours them, caring for no right other than that of his teeth.

We must arm ourselves, not using the useless vote that will always be worth only as much as a tyrant wants, but rather with effective and less naive weapons whose utilization will bring us ascendant evolution instead of the regressive one praised by pacifist activists.

Passivity, never! Rebellion—now and always.

Punto Rojo no. 3, 29 August 1909

Beggar ...

Where do you go, extending your fleshless hand, with your gloomy and dejected appearance?

What do you seek with the plaintive plea emerging tremulously from your discolored lips?

Breadcrumbs and tatters, insulting gifts, and caustic compassion: this is all you will get with such sad attitudes and means.

Beggar, it is not by bowing one's head and extending one's hand that you will satisfy your cruel hunger for bread and your fervent thirst for justice. It is by lifting your head and raising your arm that you will succeed in your objective.

Beggar for freedom ... beggar for bread ... stop at once imploring and make demands instead. Stop waiting, and take!

Crawl no longer, beggar ...

Punto Rojo no. 3, 29 August 1909

Women, Whom Do You Love?

There are beings who in appearance resemble men: beings who speak of energy, honor, dignity, integrity, independence, masculine superiority, and other things that make up their subtle disguise, which allows them to approach you ladies without disgusting you, to take advantage of your innocence, to bleed your intimate feelings dry, and make you lifelong slaves of their whims and brutalities. There are men numbering millions who only seek you out and desire you in order to satisfy their foolish vanity, to walk all over your gentleness with their cowardly pride and overflowing sense of superiority, and to make your sensitive souls pay for the indignities and baseness they endure daily from the despots who oppress them and treat them like beasts, taking advantage of their pusillanimous spirits.

Women, whom do you love?

You love a stag who employs no energy to liberate himself or you, but who does vilify you. You love a being who possesses nothing more than the clumsy courage of insulting you and not infrequently flogging you. You love that shameful individual who demands preeminence over you and who forces upon you a doubly ominous yoke, because it brings the overwhelming weight of an immense ignominy … a yoke that descends from the neck of someone who is himself subdued.

Whom do you love? Whom do you love? To whom will you give that tenderness that only a dignified and free person knows how to appreciate, deserve and conserve, grow and defend?

Ah! If you would like to see behind that mask through which the men who aspire to be your owners, or who already are, look at you ... what an enormous wave of indignation and shame would stir your beautiful hearts! What a roaring swell of infinite scorn would leap from your overflowing bosoms onto the faces of those men who claim to love you, when what they really desire is to possess you as things and enchain you to their domination, much sadder for you than many mishaps, given that they come from slaves who, sunk in abject servility, have the imprudent audacity of making you women—who should be the sweet comrades of strong men—the seat of their ruin.

Women, whom do you love?

***Punto Rojo* no. 3, 29 August 1909**

Residents of El Paso

Do you wish to rejoice in the disgusting presence of the assassin-tyrant Porfirio Díaz?[1] Do you think that this dismal bandit's visit is a great honor? Remember your history: it has indelible pages, as fresh as pond scum, and you cannot help but feel shame to think that this odious festival for him is held in your name. Thousands of victims watch you and await an expression of fiery dignity protesting the vileness of Porfirio Díaz's lackeys.

Remember at least the crimes that this evildoer has committed against you. Keep in mind that it was Díaz who paid the assassins who took the life of Dr. Ignacio Martínez in Laredo, Texas;[2] that he was the author of the kidnapping of Manuel Sarabia in Douglas, Arizona; that he is the one who has infested your city with thugs; that it is he who, day by day, with the dark complicity of your authorities, defiles with abominable attacks the memory of Lincoln, which should be dear to you.

It is probable that Díaz, though he has offered to do so, will not come in the end, because the assassin is a coward and he is

1 An allusion to a cross-border meeting between Díaz and President Howard Taft planned for October 16, 1909, to demonstrate U.S. support for Díaz's re-election in exchange for the Mexican dictator's protection of U.S. foreign investment.

2 Dr. Ignacio Martínez (1844–1891), a former Mexican general, was a favored opposition candidate in the run-up to the 1892 presidential election against Díaz. He was forced to flee Mexico and subsequently settled in Laredo, Texas, where he was murdered by assassins operating on the orders of Nuevo León's Governor Bernardo Reyes.

afraid of approaching the border. In any case, you should protest the comedy that, in your name, is being made to his blood-and-filth-soaked name.

In Mexico, those who pretend in the presence of the Tyrant have an excuse; that excuse is terror. But you do not and cannot have this excuse, and if you accept your assigned role in this degrading farce, there will be no subterfuge worth it. Not even the waters of a hundred biblical floods would be able to cleanse the stain that you will have brought on yourselves.

Maintain your dignity or wait for me to brand your face with the word that will become the emblem of your future: Wretches!

Punto Rojo no. 3, 29 August 1909

And Still ... You Remain Passive!

A woman: the wife of a journalist complicit with the regime, who cannot be suspected of revolutionary sympathies, has been incarcerated in the Mexican capital, having been placed in strict solitary confinement in a dungeon in the Belem prison, celebrated for its dreadful and disgusting nature.

Péres de León, the judge of freedom-killing sentences, who has distinguished himself as an evil persecutor of those whom Díaz-potism marks with the color red, is the one who has closed, with the luxurious barbarity of isolation, the cell of Paulino Martínez's wife, and who shutters the printing-press of *The Voice of Juárez*, whose owner is one of the most ardent defenders of the existing peace and order, but who somehow has gotten mixed up in the suffragist agitation born from the interview with Creelman, and which has disturbed the man who wanted to let this discovery be known.[1]

Martínez was fleeing when his female comrade was taken from her children and thrown into Belén to satisfy justice—for a trifle,

---

1   In 1908, journalist James Creelman (1859–1915) published a telling interview he had held with Díaz in *Pearson's Magazine* in which the dictator claimed that Mexico was ready for democracy and that, accordingly, he would stand down during the 1910 election. The interview was soon thereafter translated and published in much of the Mexican press, inspiring the suffragist activity Praxedis mentions, including that of the Anti-Reelectionist Party founded in 1909 by Francisco I. Madero.

for nothing: merely a kind word for the Army, a word of which the owner and director of *The Voice of Juárez* was not the author.

This crude and cowardly outrage, targeting a woman (who is allowed, out of pure deference, two quilts in prison), fills the timid spirits of many dupes who, singing the old and tremulous psalm of order, peace, and respect for the law, hope that tyranny might spare them mistreatment and reward their passivity with a freedom whose conquest they fear to undertake in a dignified and virile fashion.

Brutal disillusionment makes its bitter voice heard to the poor babies for whom everything had the color of milk.

Paulino Martínez's work is for peace; he has advised compliance with the authorities to a sublimely naïve degree, and yet, despite this, the Dictatorship persecutes and injures him as though he were a revolutionary or a rabble-rouser—because tyranny is tyranny, and it can never be the cautious nanny of any movement that has even vague hints of liberation.

Díaz does not like half-servants, and in this he shows more logic and experience than the patient evolutionists.

For many, many years, we have been witnessing and tolerating the Dictatorship's atrocities. What is happening has taken place thousands of times, with even darker details. Yet still there are those who continue to maintain that through unarmed and humble civic action—or action armed with an electoral ballot, which amounts the same thing—everything will be achieved.

You have seen many infamies and swallowed much shame; you are now contemplating new crimes and will see and endure still more—yet you remain passive.

Punto Rojo no. 4, 16 September 1909

Anniversary

In a year's time, a century will have passed since an epic of redemption began with the courageous disobedience of an old visionary, of a utopian who gathered the humble and exploited of 1810 around his banner of rebels.[1]

Soon it will be the Centennial of that illegal act.

The anniversary of 1810 greets the present generations with a formidable rebuke.

An immense interrogation rises on the Mexican horizon, as though it were a flaming comet approaching us at unstoppable speed.

1810 accuses; 1810 interrogates.

Mexicans, how do you respond?

The mission of those shirtless ones, rather than progressing, has been drowned in the apathy and fear of their descendants. Mexico has regressed by train far beyond from where it set off with naked feet.

Celebration, then, seems profoundly ironic.

We live under the claw of the rapacious North, and one fears provoking the anger of the senile despot simply by breathing. Autonomy and freedom are for the Mexican populace two miserable paradoxes, and yet the idea of throwing commemorative celebrations of dignified and glorious acts is still considered.

---

1   An allusion to Miguel Hidalgo (1753–1811), the Catholic priest who initiated Mexico's independence from Spain with the *"Grito de Dolores"* made on September 16, 1810.

The slaves directed by their committees sing victory odes to the freedom that has been renounced and to the courage that has been exchanged for docility.

Hot air, smoke, and genuflections—this is what the ritual of the historical moment prescribes for the enthusiasms of those who feed on illusions, and for the gravediggers of the Mexican race.

Will the sun of the Centennial burn the backs of the flock or kiss the fiery brow of a people?

Respond, Mexicans: now is the time to wash our rags so that they glisten in the first light of the Centennial of the liberatory effort of 1810.

Punto Rojo no. 4, 16 September 1909

Wretches!

The latest news has arrived to us from Yuma: on the twelfth of this month, our comrades Rivera, Magón, and Villarreal were transferred to Florence, Arizona.

The abuses they experienced in Yuma will doubtless continue in Florence—that is the watchword. In Yuma they held Librado Rivera for several days in a section called "The Snakes," which is the same as the "Purgatory" of Ulúa.[1] Rivera was gravely ill, and so the hit men of Yuma subjected him to a diet of bread and water—all of this under the supervision of Captain Rynning, who led to Cananea, in 1906, the invading troops that Izábal and Greene had requested to murder the striking Mexican workers.[2]

Punto Rojo **no. 4, 16 September 1909**

1   The San Juan de Ulúa prison in Veracruz state, where many Liberals perished as political prisoners. See the next article, "Ulúa Speaks."

2   Guerrero is referring to the Cananea miners' strike of June 1906. Rafael Izábal (1854–1910) was governor of Sonora during the strike; Colonel William Cornell Greene (1852–1911) owned the Cananea mine; Captain Thomas H. Rynning (1866–1944), of the Arizona Rangers, led the cross-border attack to suppress the strike, with the assistance of Mexican rural police and federal troops.

Ulúa Speaks[1]

Throw an evil secret into the deepest chasm: bury disgrace under countless mountains and depart from the place where you plan to leave them forever, immobile and mute; wash your face and hands; cover yourselves with gold and dress yourselves with adulations. Go on; go as far as you can, and at the end of each stage and throughout the journey, the evil secret that you threw into the chasm and the disgrace that you left below those countless mountains will come out to greet you.

No chasm can hide, nor mountain cover, filthy secrets and cowardly ignominies.

Disgusted with the assassins, the pained soul of the prisons allows its roar or lament to be heard every so often. Ulúa, that Vitellius of the coral reefs emerging off the Atlantic coast, devours precious lives, stopping only as long as it takes to vomit corpses.[2] In

---

1   This essay addresses the fate of many Liberals who were imprisoned in the San Juan de Ulúa prison in Veracruz in the lead-up to the widespread insurrection that Praxedis had organized for late June 1908. According to Elena Azaola Garrido, author of *Rebelión y derrota del magonismo agrario* (México, D.F.: Secretaría de Educación Pública, 1982), approximately 80 percent of the Liberal and indigenous Zoque and Popoluca *guerrillas* who participated in PLM uprisings in the municipalities of Acayucan and Soteapan of Veracruz in 1906 perished in Ulúa due to unhygienic conditions and torture (156, 195).

2   Vitellius Germanicus Augustus (15–69 CE), a Roman Emperor who reigned briefly during the Year of the Four Emperors

a stomach gorged with sacrifices, it feels the breath of a martyr who thrashes the tainted flesh of a Republic that still has submission on its brow and prayers for the Beast that strangles it on its lips.

The horror enfolded by the tragic dampness of an implacable devourer erupts like a clarion call to proclaim a poem full of iniquities.

In a bit over a year, a hundred prisoners, whether revolutionaries or simply suspects, have perished in Ulúa, victims of the special regime to which they are subjected. Two hundred other comrades are being quickly pushed to the same end. Among the horrible conditions under which these, our brothers, pass their days include: foul bathrooms, rotten or poisoned food, endless solitary confinement, insults, lashes, and a thousand other undignified, despicable, and cowardly things used against them with a refinement that would please the grim imagination of a Philip II or a Stambolov.[3]

With a few extremely rare exceptions, the so-called independent press is quiet, and the champions of pacifist redemption silence these crimes, while they call freedom-loving martyrs the royalist officials who were sent to Yucatán for their ambition to become part of the future Praetorian Guard of the Caudillo of Galeana.[4]

Yet it's better that they remain silent! Those timid, malleable servants for idiosyncrasy cannot protest. Their brains are hothouses for courtly flowers that spread themselves across the libertine's bed, taking care not to cause a single bothersome crease.

---

that followed Nero's death in the year 68, was known for being quite the glutton.

3   Philip II (1527–1598), king of Spain at the height of the Spanish Empire; Stefan Stambolov (1854–1895), Bulgarian Regent and Prime Minister known for his authoritarian policies.

4   Presumably a reference to royalists from Galeana, Nuevo León, who served the invading French military during the Franco-Mexican War (1861–1867) in opposition to Liberal forces based in Monterrey.

Their silence is better than their syrupy word.

Hiding within themselves, they honor the heroism that succumbs on the dictatorial racks.

And we revolutionaries do not carry out protests that are erased and forgotten: Let us avenge our brothers!

Vengeance today is the same as justice.

Let us be avengers, and let us be just.

Punto Rojo no. 4, 16 September 1909

Impatient Ones

The impatience of the present moment sinks its spur of fire into our nerves.

Our desires advance anxiously with the development of events.

The struggle has moments of anticipation that suffocate like the embraces of rattlesnakes.

We want to once again fire our weapon against the old enemy, and we are forced to hope that our firearms have been adequately tempered, so that their impact is terrible, destructive, and tremendous.

The Beast remains in front of us, and there, in the bloody depths of its perfidious pupil, challenges and injuries glow, while its claws emerge voluptuously stained by coagulated libertarian blood—our blood.

So it takes a great sacrifice to await ... to await the arrival of the moment to cut open his wicked head, remove his nation-killing claws, and kick and smash his repulsive black heart.

How can one be patient? How to wait, if they make us inhale their treasonous breath, if we are feeling the death rattle of so many, if we hear the cries of thousands of mouths contorted by desperation and hunger; if we see an entire people writhing on the ground, bristling with injustice, ferociously trampled by the Beast?

And, if impatience sinks its spur of fire into our nerves, let us increase the effort a hundredfold, so it becomes the fast steed that leads us to the realization of our ideal.

There is a brake for our impatience: ceaseless activity.

Let each of you push aside the obstacles before you; let each of you work with all your energy, so that soon—very soon—we will all be ready and united.

We are the mechanism of the clock: if we always are in agreement and hurry to march, soon we will notice in its face the beautiful and smiling hour of emancipation.

Punto Rojo no. 4, 16 September 1909

Something More

The apologies of the resigned disappear.

Relative economic well-being, with which some Mexican migrant workers' stunted aspirations for improvement were satisfied, has left their homes, mocking the hopes of the oppressed.

No longer is it just the exclusion of Mexican children from the "white" schools, against which a dignified minority has protested.

No longer is it just the insulting "No Mexican Allowed" that slaps the eyes of our compatriots in certain stores or other public establishments in Texas.

No longer is it just the "Mexican Keep Away" that has kept our compatriots stupefied at the edges of certain towns on the North American border.[1]

No longer is it just the violent insult of the racist mob or the abusive police that, inebriated with the savage spirit of Lynch, has bloodied its hands taking the lives of the innocent and defenseless.

No longer is it just that. The final illusion leaves us...

The bitter ration of bread is diminished. The mouthfuls that made harassment and disdain manageable become considerably reduced, foretelling the return of the slave gangs, full of privations and miseries, which crossed over from Mexico.

In Oklahoma, in Texas, in Arizona, and in all the other States where the Mexican element is abundant, events take place that contain more eloquence for the passive or indifferent workers than even the strongest moral incentives. Forced labor glides

---

1   Both discriminatory messages appear in English in the original.

towards us, that horrible forced labor that had remained within the fog of a memory of ignominy floating in the hovels of the *haciendas*.

The landowners of counties in Texas have held several meetings to establish certain reforms to their sharecropper system with the Mexican farm workers. The new conditions will put these workers completely at the mercy of their masters. The idea is to demand from them the unpaid cultivation of land that could be cultivated with a handful of mules, care for the beasts of burden and for the bourgeoisie's promenades, also unpaid; the purchase of all the necessary tools for cultivation, the prohibition against freely selling that part of the harvest that might belong to them; a commitment to giving preference as buyers to their masters or those recommended by them, and not others. Iniquitous and unjust! In turn, a small group of farm workers has begun forming a Resistance Union, which will not achieve anything practical unless it adopts active tactics in solidarity with conscious elements that by different revolutionary routes dedicate themselves to the struggle against tyrants and exploiters.

In Oklahoma this year, the government tripled the rent of the lands worked by some Mexican peasants. Previously, they had been charged two pesos annually per acre; now, they are forced to pay six pesos for the same land, with just a day's notice to pay up. The suddenness of this rent hike and the imperative nature of the short notice did not allow several men to satisfy the government's demands, so they were expelled brutally with their families from the land.

In Arizona, where two years ago the minimum wage was two dollars a day, the same has now been decreased in the Morenci workshops, for example, to $1.50, while, in the same workplaces and for the same work, Blacks are paid $1.75 a day, and Italians are paid two dollars.

More cases like these could be cited, which, alongside the rising price of basic consumer goods, squeeze industrial and agricultural workers of the Mexican race in this country in a terrible tourniquet.

The situation has become intolerable and it could not be otherwise, given that the bourgeoisie here know that a great quantity of Mexican proletarians, upon reaching this land, submit without protest to the conditions imposed by the exploiters, contenting themselves with being the first to become fatigued and the last to be paid.

Yet the sad apology of our resigned fellows no longer prevails. Poverty, hunger, and abuse are in Mexico. Shame, humiliation, and hunger are here. They are the universal companions of the powerless. Where will the docile ones go, or the subjugated ones, the resigned ones, so that they are not spat upon and robbed? Now that no contemptible apology can guarantee your next meal, will you remain passive, will you continue to ignore those who struggle so that humanity can eat bread that hasn't been kneaded by disgrace? Will you continue placing your malnourished muscles at the service of the slave drivers, instead of using your strength to hasten the disappearance of the shared evils?

If the ideals have not been capable of uprooting the herd mentality of certain men, we will have to await something more than the harsh squeeze that today places them between two hungers.

Regeneración **no. 1 (fourth edition), 3 September 1910**

The True Interest of the Bourgeois and the Proletarian

In seeking happiness, many people spend time devoting their strength to the defense of false interests, moving away from the objective point of all their efforts and aspirations: individual improvement. They convert the struggle for life into a ferocious war against their fellow humans.

With all the strength afforded by frightened ignorance, the privileged oppose the emancipation of the proletariat; they see it as a horrible disgrace, something like a catastrophe or the end of civilization—when it is truly the beginning of such—and a danger that must be fought with iron and fire, using all the weapons of cunning and violence. They oppose it because they do not understand their true interests, which are the same for every human being.

To steal bread from others is to imperil one's own sustenance. To deprive others of happiness is to fetter oneself. To destroy others' happiness in order to fabricate one's own is idiocy. Seeking to raise the same upon the poverty and suffering of others is equivalent to wanting to fortify a building by destroying its foundations. Nevertheless, most people, deceived by the appearance of false interests, walk through the world in search of wellbeing like this, carrying as a banner the absurd principle: profit by harming others.

In the complete satisfaction of moral and physical necessities, in the enjoyment of life, without threats or charges that bring sorrow, are rooted both the particular interests of individuals as well as those of the collectivity. Those who oppose the latter, breaking the ties of solidarity that nature established among the members of the species, work against themselves; hurting others makes impossible one's own well-being, which can be neither enduring or certain in a society that sleeps on thorns. A society where hunger walks its livid face past the doors of full warehouses; where one portion of humanity, working to exhaustion, can only dress badly and eat worse; where another portion snatches from the producers what their hands and intellects make and hands it over to the moths or useless stagnancy; in this unbalanced society, where both wealth and poverty abound; where the concept of justice takes on such cruel meaning, barbarous institutions are maintained to persecute and martyr the innocent victims of the aberrations of the system.

Heredity, education, and inequalities in life circumstances will have created profound moral and even physical differences between the bourgeoisie and proletariat, but a natural law keeps them united in a single sense: individual improvement. There lies the true interest of each human being. Knowing this, it is necessary to act rationally, transcending one's class prejudices and turning one's back on romanticism. Neither Charity nor Humanitarianism nor Self-Sacrifice has the power necessary to emancipate humanity, as *conscious egoism* does.

Where the bourgeoisie is wise enough to understand that the transformation of the present system is inevitable and that their interests are better served by facilitating this transformation rather than opposing it with stubborn resistance, the social problem that agitates all the corners of the world at this time will lose its aspect of tragedy and will gently be resolved to the benefit of all. Some will have won through freedom the complete right to life; others will have lost, along with the superfluous, the fear of losing it all. And without a doubt, the privileged of today will benefit most. In general, and this should make them feel ashamed, they are incapable of serving themselves; there are some who, even in order to eat or go to bed, need the help of a slave. When this slave is absent, they will acquire different habits that will make them useful and active beings, able to unite their impulses to the collective effort that will then be applied to the brusqueness and roughness of nature, no longer in the idiotic struggle of man against man.

Yet, if false interests continue to exercise a dominant influence upon the minds of the bourgeoisie, and if a part of the workers continues, as it has so far, opposing through passivity or treason the cause of labor—their own cause—change will be imposed by a violence that crushes those who block progress.

Regeneración no. 2 (fourth edition), 10 September 1910

Blow

The pacified multitudes made a noise like a flock at the shearer's shop; brutality, infamy, flattery, lies, and vanity surrounded me; my nerves exhausted me; I fled from the city because I felt imprisoned there, and I came to this solitary rock which will be the mausoleum of my frustrations. I am alone at last; the city and its noises remained very far away; I am free from them. I will breathe another environment; the murmur of nature will be the sweet song that my ears hear.

Standing atop the high ledge, the vagabond smiles.

A light breeze arrived; and into the vagabond's lungs something asphyxiating penetrated; he heard a strange voice moaning in his mop of coarse hair.

"From where do you come, light breeze, you who cause anxiety and mad sorrows?"

"I come from a long pilgrimage. I passed by the cabins of the peasants and I saw how these slaves are born and raised; with my subtle fingers I touched the coatless flesh of the little ones, the gaunt and droopy breasts of the ugly mothers, brutalized by poverty and abuse; I touched the features of hunger and of ignorance; I passed through the palaces and recovered the grunt of envy, the belching of excess, the sound of the coins counted feverishly by the greedy, the echo of the orders that kill freedom. I felt in my hand invisible tapestries, golden marble, and jewels that adorn to give worth to worthless people. I passed by the factories, workshops, and fields, and I was soaked with the saltiness of unrewarded sweat; I allowed myself the briefest peek into the mines and collected the tired breath of thousands of men. I went through the naves of churches and found crime

and laziness moralizing; I took from there the acrid smells of evil incense. I slid through the prisons and I caressed childhood prostituted by the justice system, thought enchained in dungeons, and I saw how myriads of little insects eat the flesh of larger insects. I forced my way into barracks and saw in their quarters humiliation, brutality, repulsive vices, an academy of murder. I entered school classrooms and saw science befriending error and prejudice; I saw intelligent youth fighting to acquire certificates of exploiters, and I saw in the books the iniquitous law that gives the right to violate all rights. I passed through the valleys, through mountain ranges; I whistled in the tyrants' lyre, formed with the taut ropes of those hanged from forest branches. I carry pain, I carry bitterness, and for that reason I moan; I carry resignation, I come from the world, and for this reason I am asphyxiated."

"Go then, light breeze; I want to be alone."

The breeze left, but human anguish remained trapped in the coarse mane of the vagabond.

Another wind arrived then in strong gusts, intense and formidable.

"Who are you? Where do you come from?"

"I come from all the corners of the world; I carry the just future; I am the breath of the Revolution."

"Blow, hurricane; comb my hair with your terrible fingers. Blow, gale, blow over the cliff and valleys and in the abysses, and turn through the mountains; tear down these barracks and these churches; destroy these prisons; shake that resignation; dissolve those clouds of incense; break the branches of those trees from which the oppressors have made their lyres; awaken from that ignorance; uproot those gold mines that represent a thousand misfortunes. Blow, hurricane, whirlwind, north wind, blow; lift those passive sands upon which camels' hooves and serpents' bellies tread, and turn them into burning projectiles. Blow, blow, so that when the breeze returns, it does not leave the horrible anguish of human slavery imprisoned in my head."

Regeneración no. 3 (fourth edition), 17 September 1910

I Am Action

Without me, the conceptions of the human mind would be but a few wet matches in a moldy matchbox.

Without me, fire would not have warmed the homes of men, nor would steam have launched, on two steel tracks, the rapid locomotive.

Without me, the home of humanity would be the forest or the cave.

Without me, the stars and suns would still be the brilliant patches that Jehovah nailed to the firmament for the pleasure of his people's eyes.

Without me, Columbus would have been a madman; Bernard Parlissy, demented; Kepler, Copernicus, Newton, Galileo, and Giordano Bruno, liars; Fulton, Franklin, Röntgen, Montgolfier, Marconi, Edison, and Pasteur, dreamers.[1]

Without me, the rebellion of conscience would be a cloud of smoke trapped in a nutshell, and the desire for freedom the useless

---

1   Bernard Palissy (1510–1590), a French Huguenot who divined the origins of fossils and applied hydraulics theory practically to transport water; Robert Fulton (1765–1815), inventor of steamboats; Wilhelm Röntgen (1845-1923), discoverer of electromagnetic radiation in the form of X-Rays and recipient of the 1901 Nobel Prize in Physics; Joseph-Michel Montgolfier (1740–1810) and Jacques-Étienne Montgolfier (1745–1799), inventors of hot-air balloons; Guglielmo Marconi (1874–1937), inventor of radio and telegraphy and co-recipient of 1909 Nobel Prize in Physics.

flapping of the wings of an enchained, imprisoned eagle.

Without me, all aspirations and ideals would spin in the minds of people like fallen leaves swirled by the north wind.

Progress and Freedom are impossible without me.

I am Action.

Regeneración no. 3 (fourth edition), 17 September 1910

The Purpose of Revolution

"Why is it that, if you desire freedom, you do not kill the tyrant and thus avoid the horrors of a large fratricidal war? Why do you not just kill the despot who oppresses the people and has put a price on your head?" This I have been asked several times.

"Because I am not an enemy of the tyrant," I reply, "because if I killed the man, tyranny would still persist, and it is against this that I fight; because if I were to launch myself blindly against him, I would do what the dog does when biting a stone, unconsciously injuring itself, without discerning or understanding where the pain comes from."

Tyranny is the logical result of a social illness, which has as its present remedy the Revolution, given that peaceful resistance according to the Tolstoyan doctrine would only produce at this time the annihilation of the few who understand its simplicity and practice it.[1]

Inviolable laws of nature govern beings and things: the cause is the creator of the effect; the environment determines in an absolute way the appearance and qualities of the product. Where there are putrefying materials, worms live; wherever an organism arises and develops, this means the elements for its formation and nutrition have and continue to exist. The bloodiest and most ferocious

---

1   An allusion to Tolstoy's theory of pacifist non-cooperation with Tsarism and militarism, based on the novelist's anarchistic interpretation of the Gospels. See *The Kingdom of God Is Within You* (1894).

tyrannies and despotisms cannot transgress this law, which has no loopholes. They exist, therefore, because around them prevails a special environmental state, of which they are the result. If they offend, if they harm, if they hinder, one must seek their annulment through the transformation of this morbid environment, not just through the simple assassination of the tyrant. In order to destroy tyranny, the isolated death of one man is ineffective, whether he be Tsar, sultan, dictator, or president—such assassination would be like trying to drain a swamp by every now and then killing the vermin that are born in it.

If it were otherwise, nothing would be more practical or simple than to go after the individual and tear him to shreds. Modern science gives us powerful instruments that have assured and terrible effectiveness, ones which, upon being used once and creating an insignificant number of victims, would realize the freedom of the people. Then the Revolution would have no excuse or purpose.

For a majority of people, revolution and war have the same meaning: this is an error that in light of mistaken criteria makes the last resort of the oppressed appear to be barbarism. War has the invariable characteristics of hatred and national or personal ambitions; from it comes a relative benefit for a given individual or group who is paid with the blood and sacrifice of the masses. The Revolution is an abrupt shaking-off, the human tendency toward improvement, when a more or less numerous proportion of humanity is subjected by violence to a state that is incompatible with its necessities and aspirations. Against humanity wars are waged, but never revolutions; the former destroy, perpetuating injustices, while the latter mix, agitate, confuse, disrupt, and melt in the purifying fire of new ideas the old elements poisoned by prejudice and eaten away by moths, to extract from the ardent crucible of catastrophe a more benign environment for the development and expansion of all species. The Revolution is the torrent that sweeps over the dryness of the dead countryside, spreading the silt of life that transforms the wasteland of forced peace, where only reptiles reside, into fertile lands suitable for the splendid flowering of superior species.

Tyrants do not emerge from the people by a self-generating phenomenon. The universal law of determinism raises them onto the backs of the people. The same law, manifesting itself in powerful revolutionary transformation, will make them fall forever, asphyxiated like the fish that is deprived of its liquid abode.

The Revolution is a fully conscious act, not the spasm of a primitive bestiality. There is no inconsistency between the idea that guides and the action that is imposed.

Regeneración no. 3 (fourth edition), 17 September 1910

The Inappropriateness of Gratitude

The abuses of the powerful, the poverty of the people, the injustices that bloody the backs of the oppressed, the hunger and exploitation that create premature old age and ill prostitutes, call one day at the door of the sensibility of a strong and just man. His dreams of freedom become extremely vehement desires; his aspirations of social improvement shore up his energies, converting idealism into action, and this individual, temperamentally ready for great struggles, arises as a warrior, apostle, and philosopher. Sometimes uniting the three in one person, he perseveres, fights, and struggles with the strength of mind and fist, until he perishes or wins the victory of his cause. Either he dies or he reaches victory helped by other men like him, determined to engage in great struggles for great ideas. If the former, either he passes into the shadow forgotten, or the fetishism of the masses places him on a ridiculous pedestal for idols. If the latter, if he survives until triumphant, the admiration and gratitude of the multitudes divert his justice-oriented impulses, and he is instituted as arbitrator of a common future, ending up transformed into a glorious tyrant. The gratitude of the people is the most fecund creator of despotism. It ruins good men and opens the path of power to the ambitious.[1]

1   Compare Bakunin in "Science and the Vital Work of Revolution" (1869): "Take the most radical of revolutionaries and place him on the throne of all the Russias or give him dictatorial powers ... and before the year is out he will be worse than the [Tsar] Alexander [II] himself."

Robust workers and selfless, constant fighters undermine the granitic base of a power that sows terror and death on the plains that groan under their feet; the mass creaks and shakes; the blocks of stone split open, and the ruin of the giant is announced, closer and closer with each blow of the pick. It will come down, but the foundation's excavators are weak; their hands bleed, their foreheads gush sweat, and exhaustion threatens to explode their chests. They rest for a moment to prepare the last, decisive push that will take down the monster who teeters at the edge of his grave. This is the propitious moment of ambitious opportunism: disguised as a redeemer and hero, a man surges from the mass of spectators who mocked that project and hindered it as much as possible; and seeing its end approaching, he strikes the last blow, winning him the people's general gratitude, which turns the rubble of the old despotism into the throne of the new, which is praised by the liberator through political calculation.[2] In the heat of a brief freedom new chains are formed. Agustín de Iturbide is a typical example of the opportunistic REDEEMER.[3]

In both cases—in that of the sincere man who struggles for the satisfaction of his proper aspirations for justice, who seeks his own happiness in the well-being of those who surround him, and in that of the individual converted into HERO and SAVIOR, due to mere utilitarian opportunism—the people's gratitude is groundless, lacking any reason that could justify it. There are actions worthy of esteem, but not of gratitude. Gratitude is born from a false supposition, the origin too of cruel authoritarian justice: the supposition of the individual free will. It turns out to be inappropriate in its manifestations, occupying a principal place among the causes of slavery. This often makes countries pay for an illusory freedom with the loss of their true rights and freedoms, so that on

2   Praxedis alludes here to Francisco I. Madero.

3   General Agustín de Iturbide (1783–1824), who secured Mexico's independence from Spain by leading the liberation of Mexico City in 1821, only to proclaim himself Emperor during a reign that lasted a year.

their shoulders—still sore from the whip of a defeated master—stupidly perches the tyrannical power of their liberators, who from this moment cease to be such and assume the role of slave-buyers, regardless of the fact that the money with which they make their transactions comes from the blood and suffering of the populace.

What gratitude is for the people, it is the same for individuals: a rope that binds more tightly than the fear and paralysis that makes the arm of human right falter; a gag in the mouth of justice; and a barrier to serene criticism, which is the genesis of all reforms.

Gratitude is the flower of servility; the libertarian rejects it because it smells like a slave-dungeon.[4]

The admiration that is a great recruiter of flocks helps gratitude, that great forger of chains, to perpetuate its yokes.

The people owe no gratitude to their liberators, just as they owe no love to their tyrants.

Regeneración no. 4 (fourth edition), 24 September 1910

---

4   In Spanish, *ergástula* ("ergastulum") refers to a Roman building in which slaves were held in chains; these ergástula were formally abolished by the Emperor Hadrian (76–138 CE).

Darknesses

The shadow is a shroud for impostures, vanity, and glitter; it is for that reason that so many hate it.

The shadow kills the useless beauty of the *precious stones* that captivate primitive minds.

In the shadows are born the tempests and revolutions that destroy but also fertilize.

Coal, a dark rock that stains the hands that touch it, is strength, light, and movement when it roars in the fire of the cauldron.

The rebellion of the dark proletariat is progress, liberty, and science when this vibrates in its fists and shakes in its minds.

In the depth of the darkness, beings take form, and the palpitations of life begin.

In the belly of the furrow germinates the seed.

The darkness of the cloud is the fertility of the fields; the darkness of the rebel is the freedom of the people.

Regeneración no. 4 (fourth edition), 24 September 1910

Let us Propel Rationalist Education

Soon, a year will have passed since the assassination of Francisco Ferrer by the enemies of civilization inside the Montjuich fortress in Barcelona.[1] The rationalist schools he founded suspended their teachings, thus obeying the brutal imposition of the Spanish Government, and their books, the source of healthy ideas and knowledge, burned in the bonfires started by the fanatics of error. Only a few copies were saved, and of these some remain protected in our care, awaiting the possibility of making new editions to supply the workers' schools that are beginning to be founded based on the impulse and desire of a number of groups of Mexican workers.

When I heard the news about the crime of Montjuich, a great desire to protest invaded me, but not in the declamatory form

---

1   Francesc Ferrer i Guàrdia (1859–1909), Spanish anarchist and founder of the Modern School movement, which sought to educate working-class children using rationalist, secular, and non-compulsory methods. Ferrer was executed by a military tribunal in the Montjuich castle on charges of sedition for supposedly having inspired the events of the "Tragic Week" of summer 1909, which saw the mobilization of Spanish troops to northern Morocco in the Second Rif War— launched to protect colonial mining interests—leading to the declaration of a general strike in Barcelona by the anarcho-socialist union *Solidaridad Obrera*. This uprising, having strong antimilitarist, anticolonial, and anticlerical elements, met the State's declaration of martial law and ultimate military suppression.

that by force of repetition following each attack by despotism has become useless—like the rage of foam against granite—but rather something that would be, instead of words or complaints, an action. I proposed therefore to the workers of Mexican *raza* the establishment of schools and the founding of small rationalist libraries, using our own funds, which are rather scarce but not entirely inefficacious, to slowly develop a free educational system for our children, and for us as well. My proposal was accepted by some groups, which have been working to realize the idea, struggling continuously with the difficulties of poverty and lacking the appropriate books for school, given that, as already noted, the works edited by the Modern School of Barcelona were burned on the orders of the foolish Spanish authorities. Several libraries exist that have a few excellent volumes, collectively put together by workers' groups of the Pan-American League,[2] true centers for social study where books are read and discussed and solid and long-lasting fraternity is established through the interchange of ideas—the product of the disappearance of old prejudices that are drowned in the new environment. Each day they progress, increasing the number of comrades who visit them and of the books that are bought by anyone who is capable of doing so.

The schools unfortunately have not been able to establish themselves completely according to the modern plan: books and teachers are lacking.

A means of resolving the question occurs to me now that the anniversary of Ferrer's assassination approaches, as many friends of his work plan to celebrate it with protest demonstrations and other sympathetic acts. Why don't we Mexican workers celebrate this anniversary by making an effort to promote modern schools? This would be the best form of protest, the most logical, the most

2   The Pan-American Labor League was a formation founded by Praxedis in San Antonio in summer 1910 that promoted rationalist education, women's emancipation, internationalism, syndicalism, and antimilitarism. See Guerrero's "Program of the Pan-American Labor League" below.

conscious, and the most effective. Screams and threats are not necessary, only action—immediate and constant action—so that our protest reaches the heart of despotism and becomes, within it, a healthy poison that cuts short its days. In many parts of the United States, Mexican workers pay what are called "school taxes," so that their children can receive education in the official schools; in other parts, there are private schools where ancient methods are followed that damage children more than help them; while in others, despite how numerous the Mexican element is, there is no school at all for their children, who are expelled from the "white" schools for not having colorless skin. Why not found and sustain our own schools where children can learn to be good and free at the same time that they taste the delights of science? With the same amount that is paid to the government for schools that teach very little—or what is spent in the private schools established following the *ancien régime*—and, if necessary, with a small further sacrifice, new editions of the works published by the Modern School of Barcelona might be made and some educators who have fled the persecutions in Spain might be brought. In this way, we could overcome the two principal challenges facing the birth of rationalist education in America.

In New York, the group Workers' Solidarity and its organ "Proletarian Culture," working together with some advanced intellectuals, also seek to do something practical, in the same sense; but, like us, it seems that they do not have a great deal of money.

It would be good for these comrades and those of the South to agree to work rapidly and seriously to advance a common cause.

Let our affection for Ferrer not degenerate into lyricism or idolatrous fantasies. His work is in the hands of those of us who love freedom. In continuing it, we protest against his executioners and we injure despotism directly.

Let our children have the intellectual bread that invigorates their minds, rather than the indigestible food that weakens them.

Free education will assure the victories that the armed revolution will achieve.

Let us convert the final exclamation of the martyr of Montjuich into a fulfilled prophecy. Let us make the Modern School live.[3]

Regeneración no. 5 (fourth edition), 1 October 1910

3 Ferrer's last words before his execution reportedly were: "Aim well, friends; you are not responsible. I am innocent. Long live the Modern School!"

Sweet Peace

"Is life so dear, or peace so sweet, as to be purchased at
the price of chains and slavery?"

—Patrick Henry

The Mexican Press speaks of bloody events that took place during
the celebration of the Centennial of Independence. It refers to the
dispersal of peaceful demonstrations by cavalry, mass-incarcerations,
murders of defenseless men and unarmed women, children wandering through the forests, filled with hunger and fear; abandoned,
cold, and deserted houses, because into them has penetrated the
terrible broom of official terror; rural gangs entering surprised villages, riding their galloping horses and firing their weapons at the
shopkeeper who had stood calmly in his store's doorway, at the poor
innkeeper who was awaiting his regular customers, and at all those
who didn't have time to hide upon hearing the droves of killers;
bodies disfigured by machete strikes, abandoned in the bedrooms,
assaulted at midnight by the thugs; women using stones torn from
the road to force into disgraced flight the tyrant's soldiers, who
flee only to avenge their defeat upon the first passerby who has the
misfortune of crossing their paths; the body of a woman riddled by
bullets, serving as food for the starving and vagabond dogs ... All
of this, amid the Centennial of Independence.

The police of the Capital city trample the protestors, beating
with their sabers all who stand in their way, regardless of sex or
age; they throw men and women in jail and brutally drive away
the ragged people outside the aristocratic places. The soldiery

of Tlaxcala sows death and desolation, sacrificing men, women, and children.

Mexico is no longer that bit of land bordered by the Bravo and Suchiate Rivers: it is the Borgia Company, dug up and converted into the fetid reddish mire.[1] Mexico has had brutal tyrants who have been selling off its lands, who have shot down philosophers and thinkers in times of war, who have sacrificed the doctors and injured in hospitals, who have robbed, incarcerated, and killed without pause—yet no one other than the present despotism has been the executioner of children and women.

The priests of Servile Peace laid their impure hands on the multitudes and debased their foreheads with the ash of submission and ordered their knees, trembling from cowardice, to genuflect on the land prostituted by crime. Barbarism arrogantly and vainly passed its flag of extermination above the withered flock. Everything was sacrificed on the altars of myth: dignity, rights, freedom, the children's bread, women's chastity, the human conscience, the future of the *raza*, the memory of the indomitable and battling ancestors, and thought, the very engine and rail for progress and civilization. The national cult had an immense altar, and the idol, grossly made up, demanded thousands of victims—no longer taken as formerly upon the battlefield, but rather in the workshops, mines, factories, *haciendas*, and in the corners of their hovels. The song of the new liturgy is a combination of sinister noises that entangle themselves at the extreme of their echoes; the prayer, the lament, the whistles of the whip, the cracking of the bones crushed beneath horseshoes, the creaking of the doors of the prisons, the curse of the assassin, the fall of the bodies into the ocean waters, the crackle of the burning ranches, the cautious footstep of the spy, the whispering of the informant, the laugh of the lackey, the clamor of adulation, the cry of little boys, and the monotonous murmur of stupid prayers …

1   An allusion to the Italo-Spanish House of Borgia, which became politically and religiously hegemonic in Europe during the fifteenth and sixteenth centuries.

Sweet peace; divine peace. We adore peace. Let us conserve peace at the price of tranquility, of the dearest affections, and even at the price of life—these have been the words that abject lips have pronounced ceaselessly into the ears of the sacrificed populace, making it deaf and destroying it, so that it cannot hear the voice of the rebellious iconoclast that tears across space, seeking virile ears. Cananea moaned with affront, murder, and robbery; Acayucan screamed with an epic and defiant tone; Río Blanco exhorted in martyrdom; Viesca, Las Vacas, and Palomas roared; Tehuitzingo, Tepames, and Velardeña spoke, while Ulúa and Belén yawned like sated beasts; the Yaqui launched war cries of agony; the National Valley arose like a bloody specter; Valladolid tragically raised its fist and... the national passivity remained on its knees.[2] Children

2   Regarding the Cananea strike (June 1906), see footnote 2 in "Wretches" above; the Acayucan Rebellion (September–October 1906), an insurrection organized by Liberals among landless indigenous peasants in Veracruz, being one of the plots that avoided prior detection by the State; Río Blanco, Veracruz, site of a strike involving six thousand textile workers demanding improved conditions and the abolition of child labor in the factories—they were suppressed by the military, with hundreds killed (January 1907); about the Viesca, Las Vacas, and Palomas battles of June 1908, see the articles referring to each in section III below; in Tehuitzingo, Puebla, and Tepames, Colima, revolts broke out following the shuttering of clubs opposed to Díaz; in Velardeña, Durango, dozens of miners were shot down for demonstrating publicly (1909); the San Juan de Ulúa and Belén prisons, to which hundreds of Liberal insurgents were sent following the crackdown against the planned uprising of summer 1908 (see "Ulúa Speaks" above); the Yaqui Indigenous people had constantly been at war with the State since colonization, and for this were targeted by Díaz for enslavement and genocide through deportation and mass-death by overwork in the National Valley and the Yucatán, as exposed internationally in John Kenneth Turner's *Barbarous Mexico* (1910); regarding the Valladolid Rebellion of June 1910, see footnote 2 in "The Death of the Heroes" below.

and women died in Sonora; they have died in Veracruz and Tlax-cala;[3] children and women, with their backs bloodied, their faces saddened, and their limbs weakened, live enslaved and imprisoned in Yucatán and the María Islands, while... we enjoy peace—tender peace, divine peace—bought with the martyrdom of those beings we should defend with our lives, ashamed at being enslaved.

Regeneración no. 5 (fourth edition), 1 October 1910

3   During the celebration of the first Mexican centennial in Tlaxcala, anti-Porfirian protests were met with violence by the State; Praxedis presumably refers to Yaqui women and children with his comment about Sonora.

Filogonio's Argument

A rowboat in which Filogonio and his companions were traveling capsized while crossing a river. Some of them, knowing how to swim, tried to reach the riverbank, while towing those who due to fear or ineptitude let themselves be carried away by the current. Though Filogonio knew how to keep afloat for a few minutes, he did not swim toward shore, nor did he tow anyone. He just spoke in the name of prudence and the common good with those who fought for their lives against the waters.

"Idiots! What are you doing? You are reckless! Do you not see that with such efforts and such strokes we could all die of exhaustion? We fell into this odious current because of one of you; now the prudent thing would be to curse and protest against it, not make such movements, because it could happen that we die of fatigue, which is the worst of deaths."

So Filogonio, yelling increasingly irritably at those who struggled to reach shore, drifted away, dragged by the river. He disappeared among the waves swallowing water, and when he returned to the surface, he once again exclaimed, "Imbeciles! You will die of exhaustion."

The story appears implausible. Regardless, throughout the world there are a number of clever and prudent "patriots" who use and abuse Filogonio's argument without appearing to be insane, but rather seeming very intelligent and sensible.

The threat from the North—the North American danger— has been and continues to be for many the most significant patriotic reason for opposing oneself to the revolution. The fear of a Yankee takeover, exploited by the Dictatorship and by certain elements of a platonic opposition and the compromised ministry, has made the Mexican people forget, in part, the real danger in which the State traffickers have placed them.

During the violent Porfirian peace, the threatening current of Yankee capitalism has engulfed the large and small interests of Mexico: the natural sources of wealth, mines, forests, land, and fisheries; and dependency on U.S. financiers has rapidly become a national fact in the political and economic orders. The will of Yankee billionaires is at present the most potent factor in the Mexican status quo. This is known and "felt" by Mexicans and recognized by foreigners. Peace in Mexico, as it is today, constitutes the most favorable means for its complete absorption within the ambitious current of Northern imperialism, which works to conserve this arrangement, as it understands that a revolution—if it did not completely remove the prey from its hands—would indeed considerably reduce its preponderance as well as the probability of absolute domination that it now has over Mexico's future.

Some in bad faith and others because of ignorance say that the U.S. awaits a revolutionary movement in Mexico so that it can intervene, sending its squadrons and troops to declare an annexation by any means. They advise that peace be conserved at all costs, even at the very price of slavery, so as not to give the powerful and omnipotent Government of Washington reason to declare us a Yankee province.

This argument is childish, and its advice naïve. The U.S. Government, as instrument and servant of capitalism, does not await or desire a revolution in Mexico; to the contrary, it fears this. All of its acts have shown this fully. Trampling the most trivial principles of justice, the Yankee State has worked to annihilate the Mexican revolutionaries, launching against them a viciousness unprecedented in its history, which is inscribed with acts of varying indulgence toward all the revolutionaries who have sought refuge in its territory and who have organized from there many triumphant or failed movements. This persecution has involved incidents that reveal the special interest that Yankee capitalism has in preventing the prevailing peace from breaking, an interest that is very far from being the simple desire of hurrying the influence of international treaties to save the power of a despotic friend. Rather it is the desperate effort of someone who fights against a proper enemy, someone who feels deprived of a treasure of which he believed himself the indisputable owner. Otherwise, the Government of Washington would not have knocked with such frequency and audacity at the door of disrepute, nor would it have stirred up with its violence and abuse the great swell of indignation that forced the investigation being carried out in Congress to clarify the crimes committed against Mexican Liberals in the United States.[1]

In the U.S., as elsewhere, there are honorable people who oppose the imperialism of their Government and the rapaciousness of capitalism that increasingly undermines ancient republican freedoms.[2] Socialism, a force that is continuously developing itself, extends over the meadows of the West, scales the slopes of the Rocky Mountains, incites in the enormous cities of the East, penetrates the jungles of the South, finds a place at the desk of the intelligentsia. It spreads through the mines, railways, farms, and factories, and rises up before Capitalism to tell it, "You will not pass." The labor unions, each day more numerous and radical,

1   This investigation was ordered by a majority vote of the U.S. House of Representatives at the initiative of representatives Nolan (California) and Wilson (Pennsylvania), and it was supported by a number of senators, including the Republican Senator La Follette (Wisconsin). This investigation demonstrated that the dictatorship of Porfirio Díaz hired U.S. federal authorities, sheriffs, and border police to harass Mexican revolutionaries, thus causing a great sensation throughout the country and obliging the media to strongly denounce the illegal acts of Porfirio Díaz, who since then has begun to lose all the prestige that, through the strength of gold and servile feathers, he had conquered on the other side of the Rio Grande [Praxedis Guerrero].

2   Praxedis refers to the revolutionary socialism that was being propagated at that time in the U.S. [Bernal, Rivera, and Santillán].

gain ground in their disputes with the bosses; and thanks to the work and persecution of the Mexican revolutionaries, the unionists have opened their eyes to the Mexican question to see the relation that slavery and peonage in Mexico has with their own situation. Cheap labor over there is the grand enemy of organized labor here. Yankee capitalism takes into account these two factors: socialism and syndicalism. It adds it to the plight of Blacks, which worsens daily, to the pending liquidation of Japan, the emancipatory ferments of the Philippines, the discontent of Hispanic America, the growth of the civilizing idea that rejects wars of conquest, the resistance that a people in rebellion can offer to the armed domination of an extensive territory covered by mountains. For these reasons, it knowingly seeks to prolong the existing peace, which allows it to use Mexico as a warehouse of cheap slaves and an endless deposit of material resources.

Perhaps if the Mexican revolution were led by an ambitious man and lacking, as it does, powerful tendencies toward social and economic reform, Yankee capitalism, through its puppets in the Government, would seize the opportunity to aid the pretender to the throne, so as to enjoy with him privileges equal to the ones it has with the old tyrant, who becomes weaker and will disappear by force. In any case, the enterprise of conquering Mexico through blood and fire would be an adventure with bad consequences.

The U.S. does not want revolution in Mexico: this is clearly shown in its conduct. The danger of absorption and conquest is not a future threat. When the Mexican people desires to obtain its freedom through the only practical means—that is, revolution—it is a present danger; it is the current that carries us, one from which we will not easily escape. We are now in the midst of it and it is necessary to swim vigorously toward shore, even if Filogonio screams at us that, that way, we could die of exhaustion.

Flocks of sheep win no one's respect. Only Don Quixote could see in them squadrons of fighters.

A passive populace is slavery. It is icing on the cake for ambitious exploiters. A revolutionary populace seeking its freedom and rights becomes fearsome to the conquerors.

Let us leave Filogonio and the "prudent ones" to argue about the dangers of fatigue. Let us swim to escape from the current.

Regeneración no. 6 (fourth edition), 8 October 1910

Laboring

Over the fallow land that shimmers in the sun's rays, with his skin tanned by the inclemency of the elements, his feet and hands chapped, the farm worker labors. Over the furrows he comes and goes; the morning finds him on his feet, and when the night comes, he is still wielding the tools to work, work. Why does he work? To fill granaries that are not his; to heap up staples that rot awaiting a shortage, while the farm worker and his family barely eat; to acquire debts that tie him to the feet of the master, debts that will be passed on through the generations to his descendants; to be able to vegetate for a few years and produce serfs who, after he dies, will work the fields that consumed his life, and to render some female playthings to the bestiality of his exploiters.

Sweating and panting in the humid depths of the mine, a man struggles against rock. Living as a man caressed by the death that the pallor of his face resembles, he hammers and dynamites; he works with rheumatism filtering through his skin and with tuberculosis weaving its mortal arabesques in the softness of his suffocated lungs. He works and works. Why does he work? So that some vain beings adorn their dresses and homes; to fill the cash-boxes of sordid misers; to exchange his flesh for a few metallic discs, which were created using the very rocks that he has brought to the surface in tons; to die young and abandon his beloved children to poverty.

In a dilapidated shack, sitting in a humble chair, a woman sews; she has not eaten well, yet still she sews without rest. While others go out, she sews; while others sleep, she sews. The day passes, and using the light of a lamp she continues to sew, and slowly her chest falls and her eyes need greater proximity to the poor lamp that steals her brilliance, and her cough becomes the companion of her evenings. Silks, beautiful and fine fabrics, pass under her needle; she works and works. Why does she work? So that idle women, aristocratic ladies, can meet at the tourney of ostentation and envy; to fill luxurious wardrobes, where the dresses will be eaten by moths while she clothes her premature old age in tatters.

Shrouded in flashy adornments, wearing acrid perfumes, with her withered face dyed and affecting sweet tones, the prostitute lies in wait for the men passing her door, cursed by the same prudishness that obligated her to put the ephemeral enchantments of her body on the labor market. This woman works her horrible job; she is always working, always working. Why does she work? To acquire dirty illnesses; to pay the moralizing State a vice tax and, in disgust and filth, to atone for the crimes of others.

Seated at a luxurious desk, the king of industry, lord of capital, calculates; numbers are born in his head, and new combinations go, far from the opulent abode, to cut off the heat of the homes and the bread crusts of the proletarians. He works and works; he, too, works. Why does he work? To amass superfluities in his palaces and to worsen poverty in the hovels; to remove the bread and the coat from the hands that produce them, and who build his riches; to prevent the dispossessed from some day having the assured right to live that nature gave to all; to ensure that a large majority of humanity remains as a flock that exhausts itself without protest and without danger.

Unflaggingly, the judge searches the volumes that fill the bookcases of his study. He consults books, annotates chapters, and goes through cases; he leafs through proceedings; he delves into the statements of alleged criminals; he strains the criminological inventiveness of his mind; he works and works. Why does he work? To excuse social errors with legal pretexts; to kill natural law with written law; to ensure that the whims of despots are respected and feared; to always present the frightening head of Medusa to the eyes of men in the witness stand of "justice."

Listening, the henchman passes the doors; his beady eyes probe through the cracks, studying demeanors, trying to discern the characteristic features of rebelliousness. His ears perk up, attempting to perceive all the noises despotism finds disquieting. He disguises himself, but cannot hide. The henchman has his own smell that gives him away. He can as quickly become a serpent as a worm. He rattles, he sways, he slips through the crowd, wanting to read their thoughts. He sticks to the walls, as though he wanted to suck out the secrets they guard. He beats, kills, and enchains: he works and works. Why does he work? So that the oppressors stay calm in their palaces, erected atop misery and slavery; so that humanity does not think, does not stand upright, nor marches toward its emancipation.

Pointing to the sky with his simonious finger and divining the pages of absurd books, the priest runs to the house of ignorance;[1] he preaches charity and enriches himself through looting; he lies in the name of the truth, prays and deceives, works and works. Why does he work? To stupefy the people and divide the ownership of the land with despots.

Dark and pensive, the revolutionary meditates. He leans over any piece of paper and writes powerful sentences that injure, that shake things up, that vibrate like clarions of thunder. Roaming, he ignites extinguished consciences with the fire of his word, sowing rebelliousness and discontent; he forges weapons of freedom with the iron of chains that he tears apart. Restlessly, he goes to the multitudes, bringing them ideas and hopes; he works and works. Why does he work? So that the farm worker might enjoy the product of his labor, and so that the miner, without sacrificing his life, can have abundant bread; so that the humble seamstress can sew dresses for herself and also enjoy the sweetness of life; so that love is a feeling that unites two free beings, ennobling them and perpetuating the species; so that neither the king of industry nor the judge or the henchman will spend his life working to the

---

1   Simony is the formerly prevalent Catholic practice of selling indulgences, supposedly for redemption.

detriment of humanity; so that the priest and prostitute disappear; so that tyranny, despotism, and ignorance die; so that justice and freedom, by rationally equalizing human beings, make them builders of the common good in solidarity; so that each has ensured, without descending into the mire, the right to life.

Regeneración no. 6 (fourth edition), 8 October 1910

Program of the Pan-American Labor League

This organization, as its name indicates, belongs to the workers, men and women of all nations of America, and their program, directed toward the improvement of the human species, has the following as its principles:

1. Propaganda and support for Rationalist Education.
2. Women's emancipation.
3. Destruction of the racial and national prejudices that at present divide humanity.
4. Participation of the proletariat of all American nations in the social affairs that affect any of them.
5. Improvement of wages and other working conditions.
6. Abolition of war.

Organizational Plan

I. The comrades, no less than five in number, who live in the same place or district can form a group.

II. Isolated individuals can also join the League by adhering to the group nearest to their residence or by requesting their membership card from the International Office.

III. Each group will have international secretaries, organizers, and treasurers who will function provisionally until the first Convention of Group Delegates.

IV. All officers will have a one-year term.

V. The initial dues of all members will be five gold cents, and this same amount will be paid weekly.

VI. The groups will create an emergency fund that will conserve their strength, giving monthly reports of the existing quantities to the International Office.

VII. The collection of dues for new and regular members will be used for the organization's expenses and propaganda.

VIII. The emergency fund will be employed in cases of strikes and other analogous workers' movements.

IX. Comrades who hold the same office can form Special Unions within the League.

X. At whatever time, members of the League can depose the officials who are undeserving of it, naming others in their place.

XI. All members have the right to initiate and revise.

XII. When the number of organized groups requires it, the International Secretary will organize a Convention at which the delegates of the League's groups will establish definitive statutes in accordance with its program.

Exposition

The Pan-American League takes as its region of action the New Continent and the islands surrounding it, without discrimination toward supporting and contributing in solidarity toward workers' movements in other parts of the world; a simple question of tactics is what motivates the organization to be regional, though based on universal principles.

For a long time, the scholarly education of proletarian children has been in the hands of the dominant and exploiting classes, which have used this to mold them for obedience and servitude. There are many workers who struggle against the masters in different ways, but whose children go to the schools that the latter maintain to restrict humanity to the path that serves them. In this way, with the enemy at home and the developing brains under control, workers' struggles have nearly sterile results, as they succeed in achieving victories and advantages during one generation, only to have these lost because the following generation has been educated by the enemy.

Proletarian education should be in the hands of the workers so that it can be beneficial, respond to their necessities, and be a true foundation of emancipation. The League will strive for Rationalist Education by founding schools, libraries, centers for social education, and by advancing a libertarian press.

In mentioning the improvement of the human race, clearly we understand all the problems that are related to this, including women's emancipation; but the League has made of this one of its grand principles because we consider it a matter of great importance that is deplorably ignored by many individuals who maintain despotism at home while seeking freedom elsewhere. The injustice of existing social conditions certainly is hard for men, but it is much heavier for women. If in reality one wishes to contribute to liberatory labor in the world, this should begin in the family—this, by dignifying our mothers, daughters, female companions, and sisters. The League will perform the tasks of interesting women in the work of collective emancipation, facilitating the means and opportunities of developing their individuality outside the deformed mold of superstitions and so-called social conventions that in many countries oppress them.

A river, a mountain-chain, a row of small monuments suffice for keeping two peoples hostile and estranged from each other; on both sides there is mistrust, jealousy, and resentment over the acts of previous generations. Each nationality seeks to be, through whatever means, above the rest, and the dominant classes, which are the owners of the education and wealth of the nations, develop within the proletarians silly superiority complexes and pride in order to preclude any union of the efforts workers separately make to liberate themselves from Capital. Generally speaking, the various racial hatreds, and above all the hostilities among nations, have their origins in the crimes of a few committed with the unconscious force of multitudes enthralled to patriotism.

Racial and national prejudices, adroitly manipulated by tyrants and capitalists, prevent peoples from approaching one another fraternally: by destroying these prejudices, the peoples will remove a powerful weapon of the ambitious. Many organizations and individuals have taken up the matter already. The Pan-American League only follows in these footsteps.

If the workers of all the American countries directly participated in the social issues that affect one or more proletarian groups, many difficulties would soon be happily resolved; strikes, reforms of all kinds, and liberatory movements would triumph easily in the region when they take place with the solidarity and support of the international proletariat, whose complete emancipation contributes to victories secured anywhere. The League will endeavor to effectively wield the united action of the American proletariat.

The increase in wages, the decrease in the number of workhours, and the humanization of all working conditions will bring with it better means and opportunities for the evolution of the workers. These small advantages, being indispensable reforms for the moment, should not be dismissed while we strive for the disappearance of the unjust wage-system.

Using arms made by proletarian hands and riches snatched from the proletarian masses, with the blood and sacrifice of the workers, wars are waged for the profit of capitalists and tyrants. The principal elements for wars are the proletarian multitudes, from which armies and taxes flow: withdrawing this element from the dominant classes, making at least some of the workers decidedly opposed to the interventions, conquests, and robberies covered up with pretexts of humanitarianism, national honor, and patriotism, we will render impossible the horrible collective massacres that the famous Peace Congresses organized by governments cannot prevent, as they are comprised of the same instruments that are interested in prosecuting them. Civilization demands the abolition of war, while we proletarians can prevent it, precisely by presenting to the governments who seek it the most effective forms of collective protest.

A people who struggle at this time for their true emancipation cannot count the oppressors at home as their only enemies; they must take into account the strength that these enemies receive from abroad. They must also do battle with an international enemy; they must fight over their rights with the common enemy of all the workers of the world. For this, then, they need the solidarity of all workers, and are obliged in their own interest to support all workers' struggles.

The League does not propose new ideas; it comes only as a new unit of struggle to make practical the principles that orient humanity toward its improvement.

Workers, meditate on the principles of this Program, and if you find them just and worthy of your efforts, organize in favor of them.

We have been united to obey and submit to the will of the masters, and the result has been the aggrandizement of a few and the poverty of many. Let us unite now to struggle together, and the result will be the emancipation of all.

Regeneración no. 8 (fourth edition), 22 October 1910

The Probable Intervention

The old question of armed intervention by the U.S. government in Mexico grows in interest while the factions of the revolutionary movement accuse one another through the rips in the secular mantle of the Porfirian peace.

With different interests and tendencies come different opinions, fears, and hopes evoked by the much-exploited intervention. The Mexican oligarchy seeks intervention and believes that it can attract the U.S. Army into upholding Porfirio Díaz's regime, or that of the successor that the same oligarchy chooses. One part of the populace, certainly quite small, fears the intervention after having heard so much from the dictatorship's journalists and other parasites analyzing the American threat. Some politicians, who intend to install themselves as the oligarchy to replace the present one, use the possibility of intervention as the strongest argument for combating the revolutionary idea, which is inconvenient for their projects and ambitions. But the majority of Mexicans, though the belief that the intervention will take place predominates among them, find themselves prepared to resist it until the end; they consider it to be an inevitable threat that must be fought until victory or defeat. In the U.S., the government and the capitalists would rather prevent the revolution than become involved in an interventionist adventure that could cause disastrous complications for their imperialist politics. A war of extermination would have to be launched against Mexico: and could one calculate what that act would provoke and shake up in Spanish America and in the U.S. itself? One part of the Yankee populace, the patriotic jingoists, who are not lacking anywhere, favor armed conquest, and they believe this would be an easy task to accomplish: just a few artillery barrages on the defenseless Mexican ports, two or three massacres misnamed as battles, in which the number and superiority of American war-machines give them victory, patrols by squadrons along the Mexican coasts, a triumphant march of regiments and battalions through the country, and soon the submission of the defeated, with domination established. Sincerely naïve and superficial people also support the interventionist idea with the humanitarian aim of putting an end to the atrocities of Porfirian tyranny, thinking that annexation would be good for the Mexican people, because in this way the laws and freedoms that exist here would improve their situation over there. The jingoists and naive ones are mistaken, however: neither would the violent conquest of Mexico be easy to accomplish, nor would intervention produce an improvement for the oppressed. Soon we will see why. A third element that could block the imperialist policy of Wall Street and the government in Washington opposes intervention: this element is comprised of socialists, anarchists, trade unionists, and free-thinkers known as liberals, iconoclasts, and agnostics. Also to be included would be the Anti-Imperialist League and the Anti-Interference League, which have begun to organize and will not take long in extending themselves everywhere.[1] Here militant energies and veterans of the diverse camps join together, where they struggle as individuals or organizations to seriously resist and even impede the predatory actions that the White House and its instigators—the owners of concessions and monopolies—seek to enact against the Mexican people.

In reality, intervention is not a certain danger but rather merely probable, given things as they are at this time. The increase

---

1   The U.S. Anti-Imperialist League, founded in November 1898 to resist the imperialist domination of the Philippines following Spain's defeat in the Spanish-American War; the San Diego Anti-Interference League, founded in early 1911 by socialists affiliated with the PLM's Organizational Council who sought to prevent U.S. military intervention during the Mexican Revolution.

or nullification of the probabilities that now face us depend on the elements I just mentioned, which present problems that should not be disregarded.

The Mexican oligarchy with Díaz, Corral, Creel, or whoever else at its head will call directly or indirectly for intervention from Washington, undoubtedly playing a double role, as it already has on other occasions, for they would not be Mexican tyrants if they refrained from villainy large or small.[2] But Washington will have to meditate carefully on its acts, weighing the national and external factors that could drag it into a disaster instead of bringing it a quiet victory and the apogee of its expansionism. Even if said factors, which these days are almost potentials, are reduced to nothing by unforeseen circumstances, or if the vanity of the U.S. mandarins grows to the point of total blindness and the armed intervention takes place, the first result of this will be the immediate fall of the Mexican oligarchs and the unity of the people, the army, and the bourgeoisie struggling jointly to reject the conquest. Part of the army, a small part, may remain loyal to the government, but it will be crushed before the Yankee troops arrive to rescue it; there will be no lack of pacifying leaders who advise submission to tyranny at home as the best way to oust the enemy, although no one will listen to them in such moments of terrible effervescence. These leaders will not offer more resistance to revolutionary activity than straw in a storm. The war will initiate an endless war of extermination, without quarter; the old resentments and hatreds that slowly had gradually cooled or slept will awaken rabidly, blazingly, and indomitably, because the stupid intervention will stir and shake them as the energies of a people long and atrociously oppressed arise to struggle for their vindication. The trench of ethnic prejudice will deepen into an abyss that civilization will likely spend centuries filling back in; the intervention will accomplish deeds contrary to

2   Ramón Corral (1854–1912) was Díaz's vice president from 1904 until the Revolution. Enrique Clay Creel (1854–1931) was governor of Chihuahua twice during the Porfiriato and also served as ambassador to the U.S. and Minister of Foreign Affairs before the Revolution.

the dreams of the humanitarians who see it as salvation; it will result in psychological regression for both peoples; and, too late unfortunately, will make the jingoistic Yankees understand the blunder they have committed, because the dispute will not be decided in grand battles: battleships, armies, and big artillery are useless in modern guerrilla warfare, the supreme weapon of oppressed peoples, with which the invisible force of the oppressed can, day by day and year by year, destroy the powerful military apparatuses.

The domination of the Philippines, despite the alliance of Washington with the friars, causes little more than annoyance; it is a ridiculous medal pinned to flesh. Vanity and the need to conserve a formidable power's prestige keep it stuck to the victor's chest, even if his face cannot hide a look of disgust: sooner or later, the medal will fall, leaving a wound in the flesh that had held it in place while rotting away.

An annexed or invaded Mexico would be worse than the Philippines—incomparably worse. The Mexican shoe is much too small for Yankee imperialism's foot; if it wears it by intervening, it will soon find itself limping pitifully, stumbling not to grand days of triumphant ambition but rather to the shame of failed efforts without glory, dragging the nation with it.

The intervention of Yankee imperialism is not just a question of nationalities and flags; it implies serious complications in the social problem whose solution is sought by advanced minorities in all countries. By avoiding intervention, a given State does not protect itself, but rather reasonably avoids a terrible mistake for both peoples.

The Revolution arrives, defying the interventionist threat; we Mexicans have the right to make sure that despots around the world do not look down on us. Lovers of justice must think of the consequences of the intervention and prevent it, no matter what form it takes, whether on behalf of tyranny or ostensibly on behalf of the Mexican people, because it would be foolishness with tragic results.

Regeneración no. 9 (fourth edition), 29 October 1910

A Friend's Advice

Since *El Imparcial* began to understand that it is impossible to keep the Mexican proletariat from becoming aware of the international workers' movement and identifying with it, it has abandoned its scornful attitude and converted itself into a friend and mentor of those whom it has so disregarded and stolen from in partnership with the Dictatorship. One editorial after another has highlighted the yellow sheets of the technocrats that address workers' affairs with apparent confidence, in order to guide the Mexicans toward the interests of the State and bourgeoisie; but it barely hides its anxiety when it mentions a "problem that we see from a distance, but that continues to interest us due to its dreadful and unquestionable significance." A dreadful problem—yes, for those vain exploiters the labor problem is dreadful, for its solution draws near through the abolition of privilege, as the revolutionary general strike gains ground in Europe and America.

Financed by Porfirio Díaz using the money he robs, the yellow sheets advise the workers—if nothing else, the advice of these editorials has the charming quality of suggesting ends contrary to the reasons they were written, true Ambrosio carbines, which couldn't be more efficient if they had been designed by Mondragón.[1] They are less ingenious than that crook Agrippa Menenius, who told the first Roman strikers the fable of the body, in which the stomach

---

1   An "Ambrosio carbine" is an idiom denoting a useless object; Manuel Mondragón (1859–1922), a Mexican military officer who infamously designed weapons for Díaz.

was the patricians and the arms and legs were the plebes, who should work to provide sustenance for the stomach that pays for their services by producing blood for them. The yellow sheets insist that those who suffer from the general strike will not be the rich, who have cars and can come and go as they please and eat as usual because they have well-supplied stores, but rather the workers who can neither change their workplace to find another master to exploit them nor satisfy their hunger because they lack storehouses or reserves of any kind. The editors believe they have found a profound and dramatic argument here, capable of making the workers faint from hopelessness and fear: why go on strike if the masters will only laugh at our refusal to work, given that we will be the only ones who are harmed? This is impartial wisdom, ignorant of the implications of its friendly advice.

The masters have stores full of everything needed to live a long time, as long as the slaves decimated by hunger resume their job of replenishing those stores with that which their masters have consumed during the strike; the masters have cars to go where they please, thumbing their noses at disobedient servants left with the dilemma of exploding from hunger within hours or of exploding from fatigue in a few days' time; the masters laugh at the strikes because the greatest harm they can endure is having the accumulation of their wealth paralyzed for a short time, only to recoup it upon the remorseful and chaste return of those they exploit. The masters are invulnerable to the paltry weapon of the strike. Good. The first thought of any worker who has the misfortune of reading such friendly advice from *El Imparcial* should be very simple. If strikes are counterproductive for the workers, if the rich laugh at the imbecility of the slaves who condemn themselves voluntarily to extreme hunger for demanding improved working conditions, this is because, upon declaring a strike, they leave—being both generous and foolish—all that they have produced in the hands of the exploiters. The rich would not laugh at the strike, nor would the workers surrender shamefully out of hunger, if they added to the strike the expropriation of the storehouses, factories, mines, and lands, filled or made productive through their labor, all due to their effort.

The yellow sheet of the technocrats is right to condemn the peaceful strike, an incomplete rebellion with null or adverse results; the peaceful strike makes the bourgeoisie laugh and is contrary to the interests of the workers, because it does not remove from the hands of the usurpers the means of subsistence and production that belong to the worker.

Regeneración no. 10 (fourth edition), 5 November 1910

The Means and the End

Tyrants and common criminals are equally subject to the natural law of determinism, and although their acts horrify us and cause us indignation, we must agree, in all fairness, that both are irresponsible. However, without making any sweeping generalizations, it can be said that tyranny is the more excusable of the crimes, because no individual can commit it without a concurrent set of complex circumstances that are independent of his will and beyond the control of even those best suited and supplied with evil qualities. In effect, could a tyrant exist above a people who hadn't given him the elements to maintain himself? A common criminal can commit his misdeeds without the complicity of his victims, but a despot does not live or tyrannize without the complicity of his, and a large number of them. Tyranny is the crime of collectivities that do not think for themselves, and it should be attacked as a social illness by means of revolution, considering the death of tyrants as an inevitable moment in the struggle: an incident, no more—not an act of justice.

Such weights and measures have no use in the libertarian approach. Science, in negating the free will of individuals, destroys the basis of the present barbarous penal institutions. We revolutionaries do not establish different criteria for the acts of the grand evildoer and the small one, nor do we use subterfuge to varnish the violence that inevitably and necessarily accompanies the liberatory movement. We deplore such violence, and it disgusts us, but facing the dilemma of either remaining enslaved indefinitely or appealing to the exercise of force, we choose the passing horrors of armed struggle, without hatred for the irresponsible tyrant, whose head will not roll to the ground because justice requests it, but rather because the consequences of the longstanding despotism people have suffered and the needs of the moment will require it at the hour when, upon the breaking of the bonds of passivity, desires for freedom are released, exasperated by the confinement the people endured, and the hardships they had always protested.

We head into the violent struggle without making it our ideal, without dreaming that the execution of tyrants constitutes the supreme victory of justice.

Our violence is not justice: it is a necessity fulfilled at the expense of sentiment and idealism, which are not enough to declare any achieved progress in the lives of the people.

Our violence would have no object without the violence of despotism, nor would it be justified if most of the tyrant's victims were neither consciously nor unconsciously complicit with the present unjust situation. If the evolutionary potential of human aspirations would find a free environment to extend itself through a social medium, producing and practicing violence would be sense-less; now it is the practical means of breaking ancient molds that passive evolution would take centuries to gnaw away.

The goal of revolutions, as we have said many times, is to guarantee all the right to live by destroying the causes of poverty, ignorance, and despotism, dismissing the sentimental complaints of the theoretical humanitarians.

Regeneración no. 10 (fourth edition), 5 November 1910

Women[1]

Children and women always have been special victims of barbarism, and only in certain countries have women enjoyed the beginnings of some privileges that occasionally place them above men socially, as in the primitive clans where matriarchy existed. But they still do not occupy the rightful place in society that belongs to them as women.

The Bible, which consecrates the impurity of women, tells us that the Jewish people treated women and children contemptibly: fathers had absolute rights over their daughters, selling them like slaves or sacrificing them, as is seen in the celebrated case of Jephthah, and the atrocious cult of Moloch, which put in practice the burning alive of children, especially girls, throughout the Semitic peoples.[2] The Jews made customary the monopoly of women by the rich. Solomon gives us an example of that, and because of this we see produced—naturally among the poor—the repugnant vices that same Bible speaks of, giving rise to the abasement of customs, whose preferred victims were women.[3]

---

1   This is an extract from the dissertation presented before the Regeneración Group during the evening of Sunday, 6 November 1910, in the Labor Temple [Bernal, Rivera, and Santillán].

2   In the biblical book of Judges, the Israelite commander Jephthah sacrifices his daughter to observe an oath he had sworn before leading a campaign against the Ammonites; worship of the beastly Canaanite god Moloch (Hebrew for "king") involved the sacrifice of children.

3   Presumably an allusion to Solomon's reported hundreds of wives and concubines.

In ancient Egypt, where the poor peasants constructed by force of whip and stick gigantic monuments to servility and pride which the wind erosion has not been able to destroy over the course of millennia, women had extraordinary privileges: they freely stipulated the terms of marriage contracts, could obtain divorce by simply expressing their desire to not continue together with their husbands, and not infrequently they obligated their husbands to serve them, precisely in the way that husbands today, calling themselves "civilized," demand servitude of their wives.

Women in India, in contrast to Egyptian women, suffered the tyranny of horrible customs: widows were burnt alive upon the death of their husbands. They were not obligated by violence to sacrifice themselves; men found a way of leading them voluntarily to the pyre by inculcating in them absurd notions of honor and exploiting their vanity, pride, and caste, for it bears mentioning that only wives of celebrities would burn themselves alive. The poor women, belonging to castes considered inferior, debased themselves with their sons in confusion; their lives offered nothing attractive.

China is another of the most terrible countries for women: paternal authority was and is despotic there, as is the authority of the husband. "The woman is no more than a shadow or an echo in the house," says the proverb; the woman cannot manifest her preferences because the precepts of modesty would be offended. She should consider herself to be happy with the husband that is assigned to her, old or young, repellent or tolerable; marriage is just a transaction. The morbid sensuality of the Chinese leads even to the mutilation of women's feet and other cruelties that are common among the rich. As in India, the suicide of widows in China is customary, although without the use of the bonfire, but with a reward of eulogistic inscriptions in the temples. Infanticide, too, is common, above all for girls.

Greek men, despite all their powerful mentation, were not very humane with their women. Aeschylus, the poet and philosopher, defender of patriarchal institutions, arrives at the ridiculous theory that women are not the mothers of children, but rather temporary depositaries for the child of the man. The gynaeceum was the space destined for Hellenic women,[4] although they trained frequently in the gymnasia. At one time, young girls came to receive special education in the ways of love, but never were they seen as the actual equals of men. Marriage was not a question of attraction. The most robust and beautiful male youths were united with the most attractive maidens, as occurs among cattle for the improvement of the stock. Children received a military education, and, to maintain themselves above their slaves and neighbors, Greek men were soldiers from the cradle, healthy in body, but mutilated in spirit, given that the Greek intellect, brilliant as it was in certain facets, remained dark in many others, despite the exaggerated praise that Athenian culture receives. The Greeks killed rickety and deformed children, conscripting the rest for battles, races, and corporal games. They made good warriors, having agile and strikingly beautiful bodies, but with such discipline the intellectual development of the race was stunted. If it had been otherwise, the mind could have reached even greater heights and splendors.

A tribe in Madagascar, the Hova, could serve as an example of good treatment of women for many of the peoples considered to be civilized. Hova women also know how to understand their situation, as they designate their female neighbors, the Black women of Senegal, forcibly civilized by the French, as "mules," because these unfortunates live subjected to the rudest and most humiliating labor.

The defamed nomadic Bedouins have characteristics to their credit: among them a criminal can liberate himself from his punishment, if he succeeds in placing his head below the cloak of a woman, exclaiming, "I place myself under your protection."

Different, as has been seen, has been the luck of the woman. Among the Jews she was an impure slave who could be sold: the absolute property of the father. In Egypt she could exercise tyranny over the man; in India she was an appendage that should disappear

---

4   The gynaeceum refers to the "women's part of the house" in classical Greece, often the innermost quarters, isolated from the street.

with her owner; in China, a victim of masculine sensuality and jealousy, she had and has a sad fate; in Greece she was considered, with some exceptions, an object; while among the Hova, the Bedouins, and other tribes, she has enjoyed relative freedom and a very sympathetic status. We must look at her now in terms of the diverse situations she confronts in modern nations.

The morality that the ancient civilizations inherited from the first social nuclei, known as clans, has been modified with the evolution of custom, as seen in the disappearance of certain needs and the birth of others. In general, woman remains outside her rightful place, and the son who receives from her the initial impulse of his psychic life will be responsible, upon becoming a man, for perpetuating the discord between the two parties that form humanity. No longer are widows burned with the corpses of their husbands, nor do fathers have the right to decide matters of life and death regarding their children, as happened in Rome; no longer are armed raids performed to provide women for the men of a given tribe, nor are children burned alive under the nose of Moloch. Established laws and simple social conventions serve as the women's executioners. Male power manifests itself still in thousands of oppressive forms; the "trafficking of white women" to supply harems for potentates takes the place of the violent raids, and infanticide, the result of poverty and prudishness, is an all-too-common occurrence among all social classes.

Beyond the camp of liberalism—which vindicates the equality of women and men—the tendency of the times, which still remains too weak to break with all the obstacles that block women's emancipation, has motivated a deviation known as "feminism." Not being able to be a woman, the woman wants to be man; she launches herself, with an enthusiasm worthy of a more rational feminism, in pursuit of all the ugly things that a man can be and do. She seeks to play the role of cop, shyster, political tyrant, and to elect, with men, the masters of humanity. Finland leads this movement, followed by England and the United States. Feminism serves as the basis for the opposition of the enemies of women's emancipation. There is certainly nothing attractive in a female gendarme, in a woman alienated from the sweet mission of her sex in order to wield the whip of oppression, or in a women fleeing from her beneficent feminine individuality to dress in the hybridity of "mannishness."

The biblical theory of the impurity of women has lost its infallibility; it is substituted by the modern "inferiority of women," a concept that is allegedly supported by science.

"Woman's inferiority?" To be sincere, we should instead say, "Woman's enslavement!"

An innumerable number of generations have passed submitting themselves to the rigors of an education regarding women, and in the end, when the results of this education manifest themselves, when the prejudices accumulated in the feminine brain and the material burdens that men pile on to weigh down their lives and impede the true flight of their intellect in the free space of the idea—when all that surrounds her is oppressive and false, one comes to the conclusion that women are inferior, so as not to admit or confess the inequality in circumstances or lack of opportunity, which despite everything have not prevented the initiation of woman's emancipation, through her own heroic efforts. Being morally emancipated, revolutionary women victoriously challenge the charge of superficiality made against their sex. They provoke contemplation with respectful sympathy of the sum total of courage, energy, will, sacrifice, and sorrow that their labor represents: this is the greatest merit of their rebelliousness, compared to that of men. The act of the Russian female revolutionary who disfigured her face because her beauty was an impediment to the struggle for freedom reveals a superior mentality. Compare this action with that of Pompey's soldiers, fleeing Caesar's troops, who had the order to hit their opponents in the face.[5] See Maximilian of Austria rejecting an attempt at escape for not wanting to shave his beautiful

5   A reference to the battle of Pharsalus, Greece, in 48 BCE, where Julius Caesar's legions defeated the much larger Pompeian army defending the Republic. Caesar is said to have ordered his victorious troops to hit Pompey's forces in the face.

beard.[6] On which side lies superficiality, stupid coquetry, and foolish vanity? Women are accused of fragility, yet does this indiscretion condemning moral hypocrisy compare with the homosexual deviation, with that infamous prostitution of men, that extends through all countries of the world and is practiced scandalously by representatives of the supposedly cultivated classes, including the men of State and the refined nobility, as was publicized by the irreverent pen of Maximilian Harden of Germany, and as was discovered sensationally in Mexico at an intimate dance of aristocrats?[7]

Religion, regardless of the denomination through which it presents itself, is the most terrible enemy of women. Under the pretext of consolation, it annihilates her conscience; in the name of a barren love, it deprives her of love, the source of life and human happiness. With rude phantasmagoria, sketches of a sickly poetry, it separates her from the strong, real, and immense poetry of free existence.

Religion is the auxiliary of the despots of home and country; its mission is that of the animal-tamer. Caress or lash, cage or lasso, all that it employs leads primarily to the taming and enslaving of women, because woman is the mother and teacher of the child, and the child will become an adult.

Woman has another enemy no less terrible: established customs, these venerable customs of our ancestors, which are always broken by progress and always reestablished by conservatism. Women cannot be women; they cannot love when they love or live freely with a male comrade, because custom opposes itself to this, and transgressing custom brings contempt, jeers, insults,

6   In 1867, Maximilian I of Austria, colonial usurper over Mexico, refused to shave his beard in order to facilitate an escape plan devised after his capture following the fall of Querétaro City and his impending execution by Benito Juárez's forces.

7   The journalist Maximilian Harden (1861–1927) infamously accused Germany's ruling house of Hohenzollern of homosexual acts, criminalized at that time; the "Scandal of the 41" refers to a police raid of an upper-class gay men's ball in Mexico City in November 1901.

and condemnation. Custom has sanctified her enslavement, her eternal minority of age, and she should continue being a slave and pupil, according to custom, without considering that the sacred customs of our ancestors included cannibalism, human sacrifices at the altars of the god Huitzilopochtli, the burning alive of children and widows, the piercing of noses and lips, and the worship of lizards, bulls, and elephants. Yesterday's holy customs are criminal or infantile nonsense today. So why such respect for and observance of the customs that impede women's emancipation?

Freedom frightens those who do not understand it and those who have created their environment through the degradation and poverty of others; for this reason, the emancipation of women finds a hundred opponents for every man who defends or works for it.

Libertarian equality does not attempt to make women *into men*; it gives the same opportunities to both factions of the human race so that both can develop without obstacles, serving mutually to support each other, without taking away each other's rights, and without disturbing the place that each has in nature. We women and men must struggle for this rational equality, the harmonizer of individual and collective happiness, because without this there will perpetually be in the home the seed of tyranny, the offshoot of slavery, and social misfortune. If custom is a yoke, we must break with custom, regardless of how sacred it appears. By offending custom, civilization advances. Custom is a brake, but brakes have never liberated the people, satisfied hunger, or redeemed slavery.

Regeneración no. 11 (fourth edition), 12 November 1910

Whites, Whites

They burned a man alive.

Where?

In the model nation, in the land of the free, in the home of the brave, in the piece of land that still has not emerged from the shadow cast by John Brown's gallows: in the United States, in a town in Texas called Rock Springs.

When?

Today, in the tenth year of the century. In the epoch of airplanes and dirigibles, of wireless telegraphy, of the marvelous rotary press, of peace congresses, of humanitarian and animal-welfare societies.

Who?

A multitude of white "men," to use the name they prefer; white "men"—whites, whites.

Those who burned this man alive were not hordes of cannibals; they were not Blacks from Equatorial Africa; they were not savages from Malaysia; they were not Spanish Inquisitors; they were neither red-skinned Apaches nor Abyssinians; they were not Scythian barbarians, nor troglodytes or naked illiterates from the jungles: they were descendants of Washington, Lincoln, and Franklin. They formed a well-dressed, educated horde that was proud of its virtues and civilized; they were citizens and white "men" of the United States.

Progress, Civilization, Culture, Humanitarianism. These lies turn to ash with the charred bones of Antonio Rodríguez.[1] They

---

1 Antonio Rodríguez was tied to a post, doused in petroleum,

are dead fantasies, asphyxiated by the pestilent smoke of the pyre of Rock Springs.

There are schools in each town and each ranch of Texas. Through these schools passed, as children, the "men" who formed the lynch mob, and in them their intellects were molded. From there they went out to bring embers to the flesh of a living man, and to say days after the murder that they had done well, that they had acted justly.

True schools educate their students in order to lift them above the level of beasts.

***Regeneración* no. 12 (fourth edition), 19 November 1910**

and burned alive by a mob of savage Texans on 3 November 1910 [Praxedis Guerrero].

II.
Thoughts

Thoughts

One needn't be afraid of the means used to conquer freedom, calling rebellious activity barbarous and brutal. It is absurd to beat against iron with a wooden hammer, although some oppose the sacrifice of a few consciences to benefit the passive, backward masses.[1]

The opportunistic and hypocritical politicians who wish to cover up their cowardice and egotistical interest with the finery of a civilization they don't even know, making a show of sentimentality and hysteria, believe themselves to be sitting among a plaza of brothers, when in reality they find themselves at the moral level of three inferior animals: the hyena, the crocodile, and the rat—because they like to eat corpses, because they cry, and because they are the scourge of public granaries.

Oppressive force must be destroyed by liberatory force, without fear regarding the fatal necessity of violent means.

Ideals that do not march toward practice are mere ideals: sterile romanticism in terms of the world's progress.

A flying thought needs an energetic, strong, and daring hand that will open—in fact, break—all the doors that close it off from the space of reality.

Death ... What does death mean, when life is slavery and shame? When it binds us against our will at the feet of despotism?

1   In this sentence, which appears in Praxedis's first posthumously published article, the author may be alluding to the conflict he had with Magón near the end of his life, as Magón did not wish for Guerrero to risk his person by joining the revolutionary armed struggle.

The present epoch is a painting in which certain characters do not fit: if it is not enlarged, it will be shattered.

To be dragged into the turmoil of the passive flock and to pass one hundred and one times beneath the shearer's scissors, or to die alone like a wild eagle above the hard peak of an immense mountain: this is our dilemma.

Regeneración no. 25 (fourth edition), 18 February 1911

He is Not Proletarian;
He is Bourgeois

In an article published in *Monitor Democrático* that seeks to improve the reputation of Don Francisco I. Madero, the newspaper's favored candidate for Mexican president, it is said that that capitalist is an agricultural worker, and that he has sweated by the side of his workers. These sentences might be useful for creating sympathies among proletarians who do not know him, but they are very untrue. Madero has been and clearly continues to be a capitalist who has never worked the plow that the *Monitor* claims he abandoned to wield "the pen of the apostle," when others had already been denouncing with integrity the crimes of the dictatorship[1] (which Madero believes to have governed only with a minimum of terror) and after many selfless people had sacrificed their lives for the freedom of the people. He is no agricultural worker but instead a large landowner, a rancher like others who have, with more or less piety, exploited the Mexican worker.

There are differences to consider between the worker who works the land and the master who takes advantage of such work. If there were not, one would have to admit that the Terraza, Molina, and Creel families are also comprised of agricultural workers because they have accumulated enormous amounts of lands.[2]

---

1 Guerrero is in all likelihood referring to the PLM and *Regeneración* here.

2 Praxedis alludes to major landowning families of the

Idols should not be dressed up in tissue paper, because they tend to sweat during processions.

Regeneración **no. 40 (fourth edition), 3 June 1911**

pre-revolutionary period. The Terrazas, for example, held fifteen million acres of land in Chihuahua. Regarding Enrique Clay Creel, see "The Probable Intervention" above.

Revolutionary Women

The cause of freedom also has women who are in love with it. The breeze of the Revolution does not stir solely the crowns of the oak trees: it passes through the flowery garden villas and sways the white lilies and tender violets. The breath of struggle and hope, caressing the fragrant passionflowers, transforms them into red and proud camellias.

Our cry of rebellion has raised tempests in many feminine souls, nostalgic for glory. The ideal conquers its disciples through their pure hearts; justice chooses as priestesses the heroines who worship martyrdom. The irresistible seductions of danger have the same magnetic attraction for all great spirits. For this reason, when the hatred of the despots attacks us more fiercely, the number of proud and valiant female fighters multiplies.

We do not envy Russia its revolutionary beauties; around our flag riddled with bullets, the workers of the revolution gather, at the mercy of savage persecutions and infamous betrayals. Thanks to the overflowing furor of the tyrants, the purity of our cause has found true asylum in the delicate breast of the woman. The redeeming struggle that we carry on has made us love beauty, and love it, not with useless platonic love but rather with an ardent, active, and selfless passion that leads the apostles to their sacrifice.

Resignation cries in the sad shadow of the gynaeceum; fanaticism uselessly shatters its knees before the sorrow of senseless myths; but the strong woman, the comrade in solidarity with man, rebels. She does not anesthetize her children with mystical psalms, does not hang ridiculous amulets on her husband's chest, does not detain in the web of her caresses the fiancé she loves; virile, resolved, splendid, and beautiful, she lulls the little ones to sleep with songs of the *Marseillaise*, lights in the heart of her husband the talisman of duty, and impels her lover to combat, showing him by example how to be dignified, to be grand, to be a hero.

Oh, you female fighters who feel suffocated in the atmosphere of ignominious peace! How much envy your spark of divine illumination causes in weak men, meek men who form the fleeced flock that stupidly bows its head when it feels the insult of the strong at its back!

You women, inspired by the igneous spirit of the sublime struggle; you women, strong, just, sisters of the rebel slave and not the debased servants of the feudal lords; you who have made your consciences independent when thousands of men still live in the fearful shadow of prejudice, when so many sinewy hands remained locked in gestures of supplication before the implacable and hateful whip of the masters; you who raise your indignant arms, grasping the red torch, and who raise the dreaming faces in an epic attitude of defiance, are the sisters of Leona Vicario, of Manuela Medina, and of *la Corregidora*.[1] You make the irresolute blush with shame; you make the vile long for the disgrace of the dungeon. How you will make the wicked tremble when the angry lightning of your beautiful pupils flashes above them, anticipating the blow of the libertarian sword!

When the woman fights, what man, however miserable and pusillanimous he may be, could turn his back without blushing in shame?

Revolutionary women: the day that you see us vacillate, spit in our faces!

Regeneración no. 123 (fourth edition), 11 January 1913

---

1   María Leona Vicario (1789–1842), Manuela Medina (1780–1822), and Josefa Ortiz Domínguez, also known as *La Corregidora* (["magistrate's wife"]1773–1829), were insurgent heroines of the Mexican War of Independence.

Flash Points[1]

Freedom is not attained by wearing the brake of legality. Each liberator has been an illegal, each advance of civilization an attack on the laws considered sacred by conservatism, the enemy of progress.

~~~

Respect the existing order and submit to the laws that make it inviolable for cowards, and you will eternally be slaves.

~~~

Sow a small seed of rebelliousness, and you will reap a harvest of freedoms.

~~~

Tyranny is not the crime of despots against the people; it is the crime of collectivities against themselves.

~~~

Proletarian, what is this life you love so much that you would shelter it from the revolutionary wind by gladly squeezing it into the mill of exploitation?

~~~

Hatred is not necessary in the struggle for liberty. Without hatred tunnels are opened; without hatred dams are placed on rivers; without hatred the land is broken open to sow grain; without

1   "Flash Points" were short, aphoristic statements Praxedis made on current events. They appeared in *Regeneración*'s fourth edition, nos. 2–12 (10 September–19 November 1910). However, as mentioned in the translator's preface, not all of Guerrero's "Flash Points" appear here; neither do they appear in their chronological order.

hatred despotism can be annihilated. The most violent action can arise without hatred when it becomes necessary for human emancipation.

~~~

Passivity and docility do not imply goodness, just as rebelliousness does not signify savagery.

~~~

The horrors of repression approach; fear is overthrown, and rebellion will respond with action.

~~~

"When this becomes formal," exclaim those suffering the delirium of failure; "when it is a sure thing, I will do this and that." And they remain so fresh in their role as critics of those who struggle, hoping that the work to achieve freedom becomes formalized, so that they no longer have to do anything but open their mouths to savor it.

~~~

"They are useless efforts. They are sterile sacrifices. Do not move. Remain still. That's it; this way you will be well-trained bipeds; eat your bitterness with the bread of meekness, so that in the end you do not die satisfied."

~~~

The multitudes follow the ambitious who sacrifice them with greater ease than the very principles that would emancipate them.

~~~

Tyranny is the best propaganda for rebellion; it gives the organizers ground.

~~~

The word, as a means of unifying tendencies; action, as a means of establishing the principles of practical life.

~~~

The right to life is the first of all rights. To appreciate and defend it, the jurisprudence of the proper conscience will suffice.

~~~

Freedom is not the privilege to choose one's master; it is instead the impossibility of having one.

~~~

What, are you afraid? Fine; is there anyone who is fearless? What is needed is to transcend such fear and not allow it to control us like the first despot.

~~~

To love life when it sacrifices itself daily to satisfy the avarice, pride, and lust of despots is the most foolish of loves.

~~~

It is quite easy to supplant an idol in the conscience of the idolaters; idolatry is not destroyed in this way. It is for this reason that usurpers have better luck than reformers.[2]

~~~

Laziness is content with being grateful, but if everyone did their part in the conquest of general freedom, no one would have to be ashamed of being grateful.

~~~

There are people who believe themselves humiliated if they do not return the glass offered to them by a neighbor or friend, yet they accept without blushing the well-being and freedom that others prepare by sacrificing their lives.

~~~

When the producers understand their interests better and declare a generalized state of emergency for the exploiters, the latter will be impotent in trying to break this.

~~~

The hoarding of land into a few hands, the monopolization of the necessary means of life, tyranny, ignorance, cowardice, and the dreadful exploitation of man by man are the sources of bourgeois wealth and of proletarian misery.

~~~

There are people who are humanitarian in the extreme when it comes to a revolution that would benefit the people, but who forget all scruples in terms of a war that serves their own ambitions.

~~~

2   Presumably another reference to Francisco I. Madero. See "The Inconvenience of Gratitude" above.

The saying, "We are hungry and thirsty for justice," is heard everywhere, but how many of these hungry persons dare to take the bread themselves, and how many of the thirsty take the risk of drinking the water that is found on the path to revolution?

~~~

If you believe that you will not reach freedom by walking, then run.

~~~

If you cannot be a sword, be lightning.

~~~

Let us live to be free, or die to cease being slaves.

~~~

In the current times, one humanizes oneself when the instrument of torture is changed.

~~~

The apparent minuteness of the star is due to the weakness of our view.

~~~

Justice is neither bought nor requested as a handout; if it does not yet exist, it is made.

~~~

Moral triumphs do not suffice for the emancipation of the people, just as spiritual food does not nourish anybody.

~~~

The same people who condemn laborers rebelling against their masters as disloyal and who demand imprisonment for those who commit small robberies moralize society by offering rewards to informants and traitors.

~~~

You speak of love for your children while your passivity prepares for them lives of slavery. Someday they will bless your love, when they are treated as beasts.

~~~

For some sensitive souls, it is more painful and barbarous for a thousand men to die in the revolution than for millions of men, women, and children to live and die imprisoned and exploited.

~~~

The whip that one day lashes the back of a comrade could another day remove our own skin.

~~~

Solidarity with others is protection for ourselves.

~~~

Through the physiognomy of the tyrant one can discern the parentage of the nation that obeys him.

~~~

To perform a thousand daily efforts for the benefit of an idler is to labor sanely; to perform only one for the general well-being is madness.

~~~

It is the epoch of oaths. Henchmen swear oaths; the newspapers swear oaths; children are forced to swear oaths, too; but as Aeschylus said: It's not the oath that makes us believe the man, but the man the oath.

~~~

Wherever oaths are used, lies are abused.

~~~

Who is more responsible: the tyrant who oppresses the people, or the people who produced him?

~~~

The revolution, with all its violence, will put an end to the possibility of wars.

~~~

There are many who await the hour of liberation impatiently, but how many work to bring it closer?

~~~

Nature still does not produce trees that give fruits of justice and well-being. Let us sow and cultivate.

~~~

Accompany action with desire, and you will have a certain chance of satisfying both.

~~~

A docile person can be a martyr, but never a liberator.

~~~

"LAND!" was the cry that saved Columbus. "LAND!" is the cry that will save the slaves of capital.

~~~

It is better to die on one's feet than to live on one's knees.

~~~

The protest against burning a man alive does not belong to a particular nationality; it is for the entire human race.[3]

~~~

No brutal punishment will stop brutal lynchings. It takes a true civilization, established through rational education.

~~~

It is fashionable for personalistic parties to call themselves "parties of the future," an inadvertent prophecy. Their future is broken, because each day there are fewer workers to turn the mill-wheels.

~~~

There is a brake for our impatience: activity without respite.

~~~

Some independent newspapers assure us that our well-disciplined army could not forget its obligations by entering into liberatory plots. I deny this. There are many officials and generals who mingle in such efforts in order to betray them and so polish their military credentials.

~~~

We revolutionaries are the clock's mechanism. If we always agree and rush to march, we will soon set the time of the beautiful and smiling hour of emancipation on the clock-face.

~~~

The workers' organization among the Spanish comrades is progressing rapidly, despite fanaticism and states of siege. Soon, working Spain, free Spain will become greater than conquering Spain.

~~~

We must work hard and constantly to put an end to the horrors of peace, so beloved by lambs and their pastors.

~~~

3   See "Whites, Whites" above.

If you feel the desire to bow before a despot, do so—but pick up a stone to finish the salutation in a dignified way.

~~~

To kill oneself for a candidate is absurd. Will those who seek only a change in masters understand this?

~~~

Written rights are only written; they mock the people, mummified by constitutions.

~~~

To instruct the brain is to make the arm's strike more effective; to arm the arm is to give strength to the brain's conceptions.

~~~

Freedom is neither a goddess who demands adoration nor a fairy who bestows gifts on those who invoke her with sweet words; it is a necessity that dignified and conscious beings seek to satisfy by putting brain and brawn in play.

~~~

Unity to obey and respect the executioners has brought humanity oppression and misery; unity for disobedience and disrespectful action will give the slaves bread and freedom.

~~~

So you cannot be lions? Fine. Then simply be humans.

~~~

Do you fear the revolution? Renounce injustice, and your fear will end.

~~~

Imagine a tiger, a wolf, or whatever rabid or hungry beast attacking your comrades or threatening your own life. Suppose that some of you have humanitarian sentiments, a certain value and serenity of spirit, and you have a weapon within your reach. What would you do to avoid the harms of the beast? Would you choose the plea, the moralizing sermon, the threat of the judgment of history—arguments incomprehensible to the beast—or would you take up the weapon to kill it—a logical and effective argument for the violence that blindly kills and devours?

~~~

A cause does not triumph due to its goodness and justice; it triumphs through the efforts of its adepts.

~~~

Behind religion is tyranny; behind atheism, freedom.

~~~

There are individuals who become habituated to life while imprisoned; would it be so strange, in this society of sanctified inequality, to see slaves who take the lashes of their masters as caresses?

~~~

A group of men has to lift a weight that everyone wants to replace, but the majority abandons the task. They march off, laughing and whispering about the meager strength of those who they left in their posts with an excessive burden to lift. The fault is ours, the blame elsewhere.

~~~

Many "men" say they love a woman when what overflows in them is a proprietary feeling.

~~~

Curse the discontent, you who love the stability of fungus; discontent is the most powerful spur of progress.

~~~

There can be water without fish and people without tyrants: but there can be neither fish without water nor tyrants without people.

~~~

Create an idol and you will take on the yoke.

~~~

We workers have no need for merciful friendships that offer us salvation in exchange for a benign or paternal presidency or dictatorship. We want comrades who struggle with us, conscious of their interests.

~~~

Oh yes, there are many thieves in Mexico. There are people so depraved that they will steal even an insignificant piece of bread when they could afford the luxury of starvation.

~~~

Fortunately for the satisfied, in Mexico there is a justice that sends hungry children from the capital to Pacific prison, spending several millions entertaining itself without remorse.

~~~

The Argentine students, gathered in mobs of fanatics, destroying workers' libraries and newspapers in Buenos Aires, have erected the best monument to bourgeois education, which cultivates brutal passions.

~~~

Alfonso, the murderer of Montjuich, has sent to Porfirio Díaz, the butcher of Río Blanco, Charles III's Grand Necklace, used by the late Edward VII.[4] According to the Court's heralds, this necklace is a treasure of art and honor. It bears the Latin inscription "*Virtuti et Merito.*"

The Revolution, which also knows how to reward virtue and merit, prepares another necklace for the Hero of Peace, made of Indigenous materials: a necklace of *ixtle*.[5]
Which will feel better on the respected neck?

~~~

According to *El Imparcial*, the sources of misery are drunkenness, intemperance, a lack of savings, subversive meetings, strikes, and premature marriage.

Our aristocrats are drunk, intemperate, wasteful, friends of colossal revelries, eternally on strike, and, very young, they have three or four women instead of one. They drink abundantly from the *impartial* fountains and yet they do not live in misery.

~~~

This world is a "vale of tears," or better said, a perpetual Icamole for certain boys of the press.[6]

---

4   Alfonso XIII (1886–1941) and Charles III (1716–1788), kings of Spain; Edward VII (1841–1910), king of the United Kingdom and British Empire, son of Queen Victoria.

5   *Ixtle* (Nahuatl) is a fiber of tropical agave or yucca plants. The "Hero of Peace" is Díaz.

6   Icamole, Nuevo León, was the site of a defeat for Díaz's forces against the government during the "Tuxtepec Revolution" (20 May 1876) that led the future dictator famously to burst into tears.

~~~

It is more sensible to sacrifice all and die like a poor rat to enrich the masters than to risk one's life to achieve freedom and, with that, certain well-being. Isn't that how it is, you sane, passive ones?

III.
Revolutionary Chronicles

Las Vacas[1]

As it had rained tenaciously during the night, their soaked clothes and the persistence of the mud that clung to their boots made the march difficult.

Dawn arrived. The sun on 26 June 1908 announced itself by tinting the horizon with a blood-colored gauze. The Revolution waited vigilantly with a raised fist. Despotism also waited, clutching the freedom-killing weapon nervously, with an alarmed eye scrutinizing the brush, where even still floated the ambiguous shadows of the night.

The group of rebels came to a stop a kilometer from the village of Las Vacas. They performed roll call. The number of fighters did not reach forty. They took up initial positions for the attack, organizing themselves into three formations: the central one led by Benjamín Canales, the one on the right by Encarnación Díaz Guerra and José M. Rangel, and that on the left by Basilio Ramírez. The barracks were indicated as the meeting point for the three columns, with the enemy between to be swept away.

The insomnia and work of many hours, taken together with the storm and mire of the march, had not broken the spirits of freedom's volunteers. In each pupil gleamed a ray of heroism and on each brow shimmered the conscience of emancipated humanity. In the light wind of the dawn, one could breathe in a glorious

1   The organizer of this campaign was Antonio de P. Araujo, who was simultaneously the director of the newspaper *Reforma, Libertad y Justicia* [Bernal, Rivera, and Santillán].

atmosphere. The sun was born and the saga was about to be written with redder characters than those of the fleeting hues of the gauze fading in the distance.

"Comrades!" cried a voice, "the long-awaited hour has finally arrived! We will die or conquer freedom!"[2]

"We will fight for the justice of our cause!"

At that moment an epic painter could have created an admirable work. What interesting faces! What expressive and resolved attitudes!

Marching toward the village, the three tiny columns arrived at the edge of a stream. Suddenly someone at the front yelled, "Here are the *mochos!*"[3] And the stream was quickly crossed, with the water waist-deep. The soldiers who were lying down on the ground in the brush arose in disorder before the charge of the rebels, some of them seeking cover in the homes, while others deserted by swimming across the river to get into the United States.

The streets of Las Vacas were crossed in just a few minutes, and battles at point-blank range started up against the rest of the garrison, which, divided into different sections and, protected by buildings, sought to halt the libertarians. Canales, at the head of

---

2   This was the voice of Jesús M. Rangel, the first to rise up on the border in 1906 to destroy the tyranny of Porfirio Díaz. In 1908 he was one of the combatants in the battle of Las Vacas, Coahuila. Later, after having served a sentence in a North American Bastille, he fought in Chihuahua (1911) against the Maderista forces and was injured and arrested, being subsequently imprisoned in the Federal Penitentiary of Mexico in Mexico City until the death of the pseudo-apostle of democracy, Francisco I. Madero. Rangel currently [in 1924] finds himself incarcerated in the Penitentiary of Huntsville, Texas, enduring a ninety-nine-year sentence imposed by a Texan jury for suspected homicide during a campaign that was launched in 1913 to enter Mexican territory and struggle for the libertarian principles set forth in the Manifesto of 23 September 1911, published by the Organizational Council of the Mexican Liberal Party [Bernal, Rivera, and Santillán].

3   *Federales*, or federal troops.

the central group of guerrillas, was the first to arrive a few steps from the barracks; shots surrounded his fiery figure; his large and beautiful eyes, normally as placid as those of a child, shone brightly. Amid the rain of steel, his classic profile stood out pure, virile, and magnificent, and his fight was brief: firing his carbine and crying "*¡Viva!*" to freedom, he was approaching the entrance of the barracks when he received a dreadful bullet in the middle of his forehead—that beautiful forehead, where so many just aspirations and dreams of freedom had made their home, from which so many noble thoughts had taken flight. Benjamín died with his head destroyed and his arms extended. He would not live to see what he had wanted so much: freedom for Mexico.

Dislodged a number of times, the defenders of tyranny sought a position that could allow them to escape the thrust of the libertarians, who, inferior in number and armaments, prevailed due to their reckless fearlessness and their terrifying marksmanship. As the combat began, the tyrannists counted close to a hundred, including infantry and judicial police; two hours later, their numbers had decreased considerably due to desertions and bullets. It was in this first period, during which weapons were fired, often scorching the clothes of the enemy, that the majority of our comrades fell.

First of all was Pedro Miranda, a revolutionary as much due to idiosyncrasy as to conviction, the Pedro Miranda whose caustic quips are still repeated by the comrades who knew him; he was action and strength incarnated in a body made for struggles against nature and unjust men—the same one who spent years working without rest, dedicating to the Revolution every cent he saved from the bourgeois vultures. His carbines, an always-increasing arsenal, could be found at all hours ready to spring into action for freedom. Among the comrades, the invariable condition of Pedro's weapons has come to be proverbial. When one wishes to mean that a person or thing is in very good condition, one says that they are like Pedro Miranda's carbines. His final words were: "I can no more ... Press on!"

Néstor López, the active and sincere propagandist, admirable for finding resources for the cause, had his leg broken a block from the barracks.

The brave Modesto G. Ramírez, author of a letter full of conscious heroism written on the night before the combat that was subsequently published in the North American press, fell close to a fence of branches, besides two brave ones who had died minutes before in that fatal place. A comrade passed, and Modesto in agony asked him, "Brother, how are we doing? Give me water … and press forward."

Juan Maldonado encountered death as he daringly advanced to dislodge the enemy.

Emilio Mungía, a coldly reckless youth, also died.

Antonio Martínez Peña, an old and constant worker for the cause, there ended his life of sacrifices when he gave himself away close to the mouths of the Mausers.

Pedro Arreola, a revolutionary who had been persecuted since the times of Garza,[4] and for many years one of the men most feared by the thugs on the border between Coahuila and Tamaulipas, died with a mocking phrase on his lips and the indomitable expression on his face. Struck by a bullet that severed his spine above the waist, he strove to reach the carbine that had fallen out of reach as he collapsed; a comrade approached him and placed the weapon in his failing hands. He smiled, attempting without success to place a new cartridge in the carbine's chamber; he asked about the fate of the struggle and through his tragic smile slowly slipped the final sentence of his rough philosophy: "The cause will triumph; do not pay attention to me—one goat dying doesn't mean the herd will be lost."

Manuel V. Velis, less than two meters from the enemy, fired with astonishing calm, supporting himself on a thin shrub and contesting with much phlegm all the attempts to force him from that site swept by fusillades. He remained, serving as a target until

4   An allusion to the Garza Revolution (1891–1893), which began when Catarino Garza led a group of insurgents across the Rio Grande into Coahuila with the aim of overthrowing Díaz.

his cartridge belt had nearly run out, and then went to reunite with his comrades. A bullet shot from a house brought down this serene fighter, whom no one had ever seen quarrel—this man of pleasant and hardworking habits and profound libertarian convictions, in whom conscience dominated temperament.

There were others killed whose names I have not determined; at the time of the fight, they joined our own. It is said that one was from Zaragoza, and that another had lived in Las Vacas, and that upon hearing the noise of combat and the exclamations of the fighters, the solidarity of the oppressed awakened in him: cinching his cartridge belt, he took up his carbine, sprang into the streets with the cry "Long live the Liberal Party!" and launched himself bare-chested against the soldiers of despotism. A fusillade left him in the middle of the street.

For a long five hours the combat lasted. After the first two, the shots from the tyrannists were no longer as deadly; their pulse had notably changed, regardless of the fact that some dashed toward cover. The libertarian carbines spoke eloquently. The barrel of a Mauser would appear, and within ten seconds the wood of the box jumped, reduced to matchsticks by the Winchester bullets. A military cap would appear somewhere and would soon be turned into a sieve by the 30-30s. The libertarians were decimated; there were many injured; but their advance was powerful, and their valor great. Díaz Guerra fought in the front lines with his revolver; his many years in exile had suddenly became the light and bold age of the *guerrillero* of the Intervention.[5] A fragment of a bullet injured him in the jaw, while another fired at him point-blank from a window penetrated his arm. That wound resulted in the burning of a home. Non-combatants were advised to leave, and the edifice was set alight. Meanwhile, Rangel maintained an unequal struggle: only barely did he hold in checkmate a group of soldiers, led by a sergeant, who trimmed Rangel's furious leonine figure with the whistling steel of their rifles.

5   The French Intervention of 1861–1867, which temporarily installed Maximilian I as Emperor.

Everywhere, scenes of heroism unfolded among the volunteers for freedom. Each man was a hero; each hero an epic painting driven by the epic wind.

A youth, blonde as a Scandinavian, ran from one danger to another with his clothes torn and bloody; a shot had touched his shoulder, another a leg below the knee, a third in the thigh, and a fourth hit him in a rib above his cartridge belt. The force knocked him down. But the freedom-killing projectile had found in its path the steel of libertarian bullets and ricocheted, leaving intact the life of the courageous youth who, regaining his footing, pressed on with the fight.

Calixto Guerra, injured as he was, maintained his position with admirable courage and energy.

A group of eight soldiers and a sergeant found themselves cut off from their colleagues and assaulted on the flank by the rebel's fire. Beside them was the barracks, but to reach them, the soldiers would have to cross a street controlled by four rebels.

Determined to leave the untenable position into which he had been forced by one of the libertarians' sudden charges, the sergeant appeared in the street waving a white handkerchief to signify peace, followed by the soldiers carrying their rifles with the butts up; the rebels believed that they were surrendering and allowed them to advance. But suddenly, when the treasonous thugs were near the door of the barracks, they turned their rifles and fired on those who had spared them.

No more than three fired without effect and ran to enter the barracks, but they did not succeed. The bullets of the 30-30s prevented them from ever repeating their cowardly scheme.

In the barracks there was a heap of corpses; others were seen in the streets. Bullet-holes were everywhere. Houses presented a bleak appearance. It was after ten o'clock; the libertarians' ammunition was exhausted; the soldiers of tyranny numbered fewer than fifteen, quartered in the houses where families lived; the rest had died or deserted. The captain, being chief of the garrison, tenaciously defended himself with the sad valor of servile loyalty. This would have ended in a complete triumph for the revolutionaries, but ... there was no ammunition. Rangel made another effort: having four bullets in his revolver and some comrades alongside him, he attempted a decisive attack. He advanced a bit and was shot in the thigh—this was the last libertarian blood shed on that tremendous day.

The retreat was initiated; step-by-step the survivors reunited and abandoned the village. No one wanted to leave behind a victory that was theirs, amid the corpses of so many comrades. But ... there was no ammunition. One rebel refused to leave; he still had some cartridges, and would not leave with the rest until completing the triumph. He found a place and alone remained facing the enemy until three o'clock.

His carbine and cartridges emptied, he left, being untouched by bullets, to continue the struggle for emancipation.

Later the name of this hero, and of those of all those who participated in the action of Las Vacas, will be heard when we speak of sacrifices and greatness.

"A failure," murmur some voices.

"An example, a lesson, a stimulus—the immortal episode of a revolution that will triumph," says logic.

Regeneración no. 2 (fourth edition), 10 September 1910

Viesca

The organization of this upsurge had been laborious work executed amid great difficulties and dangers. The indiscretion and cowardice of the masses, the vigilance of the authorities supported by the dirty work of spies and informants, the lack of monetary resources—all of this was overcome or avoided by the revolutionaries of the Viesca group. Their organization acquired vigor and consistency through the constant momentum employed by a few of these libertarian workers. One by one they collected weapons for the group: one day it was a pistol, another a carbine. They slowly furnished themselves with ammunition. Double privation had to be imposed to work three times as hard as normal to pay a few coins more than necessary to cover the right to live; but in the end, when the date of insurrection approached, they had some elements that were extremely valuable considering the miserable conditions that surround all principled fighters.

The Revolution has never had capital. The rich have difficulty serving the struggles for human emancipation; at the most, they risk a certain part of their capital in this or that political game. They are suicidal egoists who want even unnecessary things for themselves, even if their excess causes them to explode. For this reason, Tolstoy and Kropotkin are two extraordinary figures for the times.[1]

The night of 24–25 June [1908], the anniversary of the murders in Veracruz,[2] was the designated date to initiate rebellion

1 Given, that is, that both these anarchists were aristocrats.
2 An allusion to the execution in Veracruz of nine Liberal

in different parts of the country. The Viesca group enlisted themselves silently; they had taken extensive precautions; but all of them together could not prevent their work becoming evident, so clearly and threateningly that the principal local authorities fled terrified on the eve of the uprising. Furthermore, the betrayal of Casas Grandes revealed to the government the existence of a vast conspiracy, and—what was most important for the success of its plans—the very date on which the rebel attack would commence.[3]

The telegraph had communicated hurried orders to all the villages and cities, so that the civilian and military authorities would do everything possible to suffocate the Revolution, while an ambassador was prepared to present himself in Washington to request the most shameful support in favor of Mexican tyranny.

The comrades met at midnight assigning each one their place, and the work commenced. The police sought to resist; a cross-fire followed that injured one person on each side and killed one of the gendarmes. The jail was then opened all the way, so that no one was left inside. The Liberal Program was proclaimed, and the power of the Dictatorship was declared null and void.

A requisition of horses was carried out, and the scarce funds that were in the public coffers were appropriated. The Revolution took complete control of the town, without a single case of violence or abuse of families or neutral persons.

José Lugo, who had not participated in the preparatory activities, became very active at the moment of action.

The denunciation paralyzed the movement of many groups, while others that could have risen up at the opportune time failed in their obligations of solidarity, maintaining a shameful silence.[4]

supporters of Sebastián Lerdo de Tejada, as ordered by Díaz himself.

3   According to Bernal, Rivera, and Santillán, the Casas Grandes PLM cell was one of the largest in the run-up to the planned 1908 insurrection. Precisely how it betrayed the cause is unclear.

4   This is presumably another reference to the betrayal of which Praxedis accuses the Casas Grandes cell.

The government began to deploy troops to the Laguna region, and then the flood of slander and insult came down on the brave insurgents of Viesca. Hacks who boast of being liberal and friends of the proletariat undertook the task of raising the blind hatred of national patriotism against the rebels.[5] Sometimes it was insinuated—while other times assured—that the revolutionaries' weapons had been provided by the United States, which, avidly desiring to become the owner of Mexico, launched to mutiny a few bad, treasonous, or deluded Mexicans who were compared with those of Panama, being bandits and outlaws. The most benign epithet applied to them was rabble-rouser.

In this way, the "friends of the people" showed who they are and what they value. They sought with their poor declamations to facilitate the crushing of dignified people by the mercenaries of power and the ignorant patriotism of the masses. The brutality of repression could be exercised against them as broadly as despotism wished; there were now among the same liberals those who condemned the few who, being ashamed of the flock, had broken with passivity and docility. But these voices that carried all the notes of base passions—those whispers that were the grumbling of an envious impotence—expired upon reaching the ears of the pariahs, the brothers of the rebellious "bandits."

Despite the cowardice, abjection, and the debasement that depress the character of the masses, the calumnies of the "friends of the people" were not entirely believed. In general, the bold ones, who knew how to resolutely employ the power that frightens the despicable, were loved and admired. The evacuation of Viesca was ordered; the volunteers for freedom left the precinct, bid farewell by the loving and hopeful gazes of the proletarian women, whose sympathies deliriously had awakened for these transformers of peace and order, who carried on their indomitable backs the title

5   As took place with the uprising prepared by the Revolutionary Council from Los Angeles, California, to take Baja California and from there prosecute the emancipatory Revolution toward the center of the country [Bernal, Rivera, and Santillán].

of bandits, a title that all initiators of reform have carried and that liberators of all time have merited.

Toward the range of friendly mountains their steps headed. There the nucleus broke, obeying a new plan: the group fragmented into units that projected in all directions to go and create new rebellious organizations, repeating the biological phenomenon of certain zoological species that reproduce themselves through their fragments.

Viesca introduced characters such as Lugo and others whose names it is not yet time to mention.

Viesca unmasked the liberals of convenience and excluded from the Revolution elements damaged by fear or incompetence.

In 1908, the troops of tyranny did not triumph anywhere. Treachery crushed the triumph of the revolution: that is all.

Regeneración **no. 3 (fourth edition), 17 September 1910**

Palomas

This chapter of libertarian history should be entitled "Francisco Manrique" to commemorate that youth, nearly a child, who was killed by tyranny's bullets on 1 July 1908, in the frontier village of Palomas. The events trace his silhouette above the hazy depths of this semi-unknown day, fading away in the gray panorama of the desert.

Only eleven libertarians could come together when persecution fell like hail on the revolutionary fields.[1] Eleven and no more attempted with a bold move to save the revolution that appeared to flounder in the rough waters of betrayal and cowardice.

The red dawn of Las Vacas had already shone, and Viesca, evacuated by the revolution, resounded still with the subversive cry of our "bandits," when this tiny group formed amid repressive violence and launched itself with a fistful of cartridges and a few bombs, hurriedly constructed with substandard materials, against an enemy that was prepared to receive it with countless elements of resistance; against a tyranny strengthened by stupidity, fear, and disloyalty; against the secular despotism that sinks its heels into the disgraceful rug of still backs known as national passivity.

Palomas was found on the path that the group was supposed to follow; its capture was unimportant for the development of the

1 Among those participating in the action were Praxedis G. Guerrero, Francisco Manrique, Enrique Flores Magón, Manuel Banda, and José Inés Salazar. The last of these subsequently betrayed the Revolution by joining Victoriano Huerta [Bernal, Rivera, and Santillán].

adopted strategic plan, but it was advisable to terrify the rural and judicial police guards who had a garrison there, so that the group crossing the desert would not be bothered by surveillance.

On the way, the telegraph lines were cut section by section.

With their carbines held tightly and ready to fire, their *sombreros* pushed back, their steps cautious but firm, ears attentive to every sound, and brows furrowed to concentrate the visual ray that fought with the blackness of night, the eleven revolutionaries arrived at the vicinity of the Customs House. Two bombs thrown at it showed that the building was empty. The rural and judicial police guards, forcing local men to take up arms, had holed themselves up in the barracks. Before the attack, the libertarians checked the houses along the way so that no enemies were left in the rear, reassuring the women in passing and explaining to them the object of the revolution in brief sentences.

Soon their hands touched the adobe of the barracks, and soon the battlements and rooftops showed, through the muzzle-flashes of rifles, the number of defenders. Inside there were twice or more the number of men outside. The struggle started on unequal terms for those who arrived. The adobe walls were a magnificent defense against Winchester bullets, and the bombs that would have resolved the situation in just a few moments turned out to be too small.

Francisco Manrique, the first to face all dangers, advanced toward the door of the barracks; fighting bare-chested two steps from the treasonous battlements spitting lead and steel, he fell, mortally wounded.

The struggle continued, with bullets continuing to whistle from above downward and from below upward. The horizon turned pale with the approaching sun, and Pancho also grew pale, invaded by the death which advanced through the body that had been proud, agile, and reckless just a few hours before.[2] The day began, blurring its paleness with that of the fading revolutionary star.

It was necessary to continue the march toward the heart of the mountain ranges. It was imperative to quickly bring the fire

2   "Pancho" is a common nickname for Francisco.

of rebellion to every possible place.

The final bomb served to destroy a door and take some horses. Pancho, unconscious, appeared to have died.

The cause had sacrificed the life of an exceptional fighter, and that same cause cruelly required the abandonment of his body in front of those adobe walls splattered with his blood, spectators of his agony, witnesses of his final beautiful act of sublime stoicism.

Pancho regained consciousness shortly after the retreat of his ten comrades. He was interrogated, and he had the serenity of answering everything, attempting with his words to indirectly help his friends. He remained incognito until death, thinking lucidly that if his real name were known, despotism could, by deducing who had accompanied him, ensure their annihilation if the revolution were defeated. From him, they learned neither plots, nor names: nothing to serve tyranny.

Pancho loved truth. He never lied to avoid responsibility or benefit himself. His word was frank and loyal, sometimes crude, but always sincere. And he, who had spurned life and well-being bought with falsity, died lying: a sublime lie, wrapped in the anonymity of a conventional name—Otilio Madrid—to save the revolution and his comrades.

I had known Pancho since childhood. At school we sat at the same bench. During adolescence, we made pilgrimages together through exploitation and poverty, and later our ideals and our efforts joined together in revolution. We were brothers as few brothers can be. No one penetrated the beauty of his feelings as I did. He was a profoundly good youth, despite having a nature as untamed as the tempestuous sea.

Pancho renounced the work that he had at the Treasury of the State of Guanajuato to become a worker and later a dedicated paladin of freedom, at whose altar he sacrificed his existence, so full of intense squalls and enormous pain, which he knew how to tame with his diamond will. His two great loves were his kind and excellent mother and freedom. He lived in poverty, suffering from bourgeois exploitation and injustice, because he wanted to be neither bourgeois nor exploiter. When his father died, he renounced the inheritance left to him. Though he could have lived off a governmental post, he became the State's enemy and struggled against it from the summit of his voluntary and proud poverty. He was a rebel of the moral type of Bakunin: action and idealism joined together in his brain. Wherever the revolution needed his activity, he went there, whether he had money or not, because he knew how to open paths by force of astuteness, energy, and sacrifice.

That was Otilio Madrid, whom they called the "ringleader" of the "bandits" of Palomas. That was the man who lived for truth and expired shrouded in a sublime lie and on whose pale lips palpitated two names during his final moments: that of his beloved mother and that of my own, his brother who still lives to do justice to his memory and to continue the struggle for which he shed his blood; who lives to address the passivity of a people with the heroic and youthful silhouette of the one sacrificed at Palomas.

How many were the men from the government who died in that combat? Tyranny knows how to cover that up.

Nature has allied itself with despotism.

The group was defeated by that terrible Amazon of the desert: thirst, a flame that embraces, a serpent that strangulates, an anxiety that makes one mad—the voluptuous companion of the restless and soft dunes ... Neither the sword nor the rifle ... Thirst, with the indescribable grimace of its caresses, burning the lips with its kisses, horribly drying out the tongue with its ardent breath, furiously scratching the throat, it halted those atoms of rebellion ... And, in the distance, the mirage of a crystalline lake laughing at the thirsty man who dragged himself, clutching a carbine, impotent to fight against the wild Amazon of the desert, rabidly biting the ashen grass that provided neither shade nor juice.

Regeneración no. 4 (fourth edition), 24 September 1910

The Death of the Heroes

Following the shudder of Viesca, the prisons received an abundant supplement of guests. Besides the elder and the man arrived the adolescent to sink into the dimly lit dungeons. Rebels and those suspected of rebellion piled up confused in the infected facility of prison. After the spy and the soldier came the judge with the sentence in his pocket. The guilty ones appeared to respond to the charges against them before the prison-bars of despotism. The juridical process developed—a process like all others that are characterized by blindness, fear, and passion. The sentences were pronounced.

Lorenzo Robledo: twenty years' imprisonment.
Lucio Chaires: fifteen years.
Juan B. Hernández: fifteen years.
Patricio Plendo: fifteen years.
Félix Hernández: fifteen years.
Gregorio Bedolla: fifteen years.
Leandro Rosales: fifteen years.
José Hernández: fifteen years.
Andrés Vallejo: fifteen years.
Juan Montelongo: three years.
Julián Cardona: fifteen years.

All eleven of them, to be sent to Ulúa—to the old Ulúa, of inquisitorial barrels.[1]

---

1 Most likely a reference to the barrel pillory, a torture device sometimes known as the "Spanish mantle."

José Lugo received the death penalty. His vigorous youth, his boldness, his pleasant and resolute personality wounded the irascible minds of the executioners. They would shoot the Revolution in the breast of that youth, so courageous and fiery.

The coldness of his corpse would extinguish the sparking ember.

Lugo confronted the consequences of his libertarian action without perturbation; he refused to inform on his comrades and slapped with his word of freedom and justice the hitmen who sent him to the gallows. The execution was delayed, and Lugo spent long months imprisoned, waiting daily for death with the calmness of the conscious, treating with fraternal goodness the friend who had clumsily handed him over to the oppressors. Neither recrimination nor complaint emerged from his lips.

Mighty was that youth who frightened his judges with the greatness of his character.

In the end came the moment that despotism believed to be opportune, and José Lugo was driven to a farmyard; they wanted to blindfold him, but he scornfully rejected this offer. He stood upright, serene, without altering his pulse in front of the squadron of pale soldiers, who fired their weapons at his heroic breast.

Later, the slab: the savage exhibition of a corpse riddled by bullets to terrorize the spirits of others. His desolate mother; the weakest tyranny; the Revolution upright. José Lugo is immortal! This is a date we will not forget: 3 August 1908. The fiery Yucatec Siberia had a beautiful jolt of rebellious energies; its vibrations still fill the tragic aridity of its steppes. The HYDRA, cut up in pieces, is reproduced in each one of them.

After Valladolid, the events that shook Viesca repeat themselves: the swelling of prisons, absurd persecutions, useless murders, and repressive cowardly cruelties.

Ramírez Bonilla, Kankum, and Albertos were taken violently to a War Council:[2] justice there was not the cunning and under-

2   Maximiliano Ramírez Bonilla, Atilano Albertos, and José E. Kantún were militant opponents of Díaz who helped organize the

handed shyster, but rather the uniformed beast. Quickly, with the accusatory rapidity of official panic, a summary execution was pronounced, and the three rebels received death penalties, as they did not wish to dedicate their lives to submission and servility.[3] Their magnificent serenity did not change upon hearing the verdict. Two of them called their fiancées to hold their weddings beside the gallows: strong women, dignified comrades of these valiant ones! Life palpitated intensely above the abyss that opened.

Ramírez Bonilla, Kankum, and Albertos rolled on the ground in front of the fateful scene to arise as lessons in strength and rebellion. Later came the mourning of widows. The vile newspapers applauded the acts or rationalized justice; tyranny agonized.

The Revolution marches! A new error hastens the unhinging of the old world.

And the people...?

Ah! If Lugo, Albertos, Ramírez Bonilla, and Kankum do not move the conscience of Mexicans, I will deny this people even the contempt of my spit!

Regeneración no. 1 (fourth edition), 3 September 1910

---

insurrection of 1,500 peasants in Valladolid, Yucatán, on 4–9 June, 1910.

3 Presumably because they were offered an alternative life sentence of hard labor.

IV.
Magón's Reminisces

Praxedis G. Guerrero Has Died

The latest news from our representative in El Paso, Texas, confirms the rumors that had been circulating about the fate of the secretary of the Organizational Council of the Mexican Liberal Party, Praxedis G. Guerrero, in the mountains of Chihuahua.

Guerrero has died, says the Council's delegate. During the glorious fight in Janos, the young libertarian Praxedis G. Guerrero bid his farewell to life.

Praxedis has died and I still do not want to believe it. I have collected data, received information, analyzed these data, and scrutinized such information in the most severely critical light. Everything tells me that Praxedis no longer lives, and that he has died; but against my deductions from reason rises floods of lamentation that cry: "No, Praxedis has not died; the beloved brother still lives… "

I see him everywhere and at all times; sometimes I believe I will find him working in the office in his favorite places, but upon reminding myself of his eternal absence, I feel a knot in my throat. The brother who was so good and so generous has left.

I recall his words, which were as highly developed as his thought. I recall the confidence in which he held me. "I do not believe that I will survive this Revolution," the hero would tell me with a frequency that filled me with anguish. I also believed that he would die soon. He was so brave!

Praxedis was a tireless worker. I never heard from his lips a complaint regarding the fatigue induced by his hard labor. He was always seen bent over his work-table, writing, writing, writing those luminous articles that honor the revolutionary literature of

Mexico—articles immersed in sincerity, being extremely beautiful for their form and profound meaning. Often he would tell me, "How poor is language; there are no terms that translate exactly what one thinks; thought loses much of its vitality and beauty in being put to paper."

And still, that extraordinary man knew how to create true artworks with the crude materials of language.

Being a selfless and extremely modest man, he wanted nothing for himself. Several times we insisted that he buy himself dress clothes, but never did he accept. "Everything for the cause," he would say, smiling. Once, seeing that he was losing weight quickly, I advised him to eat better, considering that he lived off just a few legumes. He replied, "I could not tolerate rewarding myself with better food when millions of human beings do not at this moment even have a piece of bread to place in their mouths."

All this he said with the sincerity of the apostle, with the simplicity of a true saint. There was no pretense in him. His high and luminous forehead reflected all his thoughts. Praxedis came from one of the rich families in Guanajuato State. Together with his brothers, he inherited a *hacienda*. With the products of that *hacienda* he could have lived comfortably in idleness, but before everything else, he was a libertarian. What right did he have to deprive the farmhands of the product of their labor? What right did he have to hold in his hands the land that the workers irrigated with their sweat? Praxedis renounced his inheritance and came to unite himself with his brothers, the workers, to gain with his own hands the piece of bread to take to his mouth without the remorse of securing it through the exploitation of his fellow humans.

Praxedis was nearly a child when, after having renounced luxury, wealth, and the nearly beastly satisfactions of the bourgeoisie, he adopted manual labor. He did not enter the proletarian ranks as one defeated in the struggle for existence, but rather as a gladiator who enlisted in the proletariat to place his effort and great brain at the service of the oppressed. He was not a ruined man who saw it necessary to take up the pick and the shovel to survive, but rather the apostle of a grand idea who voluntarily renounced the pleasures of life to propagate by means of example what he thought.

And *El Imparcial* refers to this magnificent man as a bandit: in large font that despicable rag, upon learning of the events in Janos, reports that there died "the fearsome bandit Guerrero."

Bandit? Then, what is the definition of a good man? Oh, rest in peace, beloved brother! Perhaps I am destined to be your avenger.

In speaking of Praxedis G. Guerrero, it is impossible not to mention that other hero who fell, riddled by the bullets of the henchmen during the glorious action of Palomas during the summer of 1908... Do you remember him? He was called Francisco Manrique, another youth from Guanajuato who also renounced his inheritance so as not to exploit his fellow humans. Praxedis and Francisco, a beautiful couple of dreamers, were inseparable comrades whom only death could separate—but only for a short while ...

Praxedis was the spirit of the libertarian movement. Without vacillation, I can say that Praxedis was the most pure, most intelligent, and most selfless man, the bravest when it came to the cause of the dispossessed. The gap that he leaves behind may well never be filled. Where to find a man without any type of ambition, being fully brain and heart, brave and active like him?

The proletariat perhaps has not realized the enormous loss it has suffered. Without hyperbole it can be said that it is not just Mexico that has lost the best of its sons, but also humanity itself that has suffered this loss, because Praxedis was a libertarian.

And still I cannot believe the terrible reality. Every so often I feel that a consoling telegram will arrive, reporting that Praxedis lives. The brutal truth cannot annihilate in the depths of my heart a remainder of hope that burns like an oil lamp that is about to be extinguished. My tortured spirit believes that it will still find him in his favorite places—in the office, where he and I dreamed so much about the beautiful morning of social emancipation—the martyr, bent over his work-table, writing, writing, writing.

Regeneración no. 20 (fourth edition), 14 January 1911

Praxedis G. Guerrero

It was a year ago that the young anarchist Praxedis G. Guerrero, secretary of the Organizational Council of the Mexican Liberal Party, died in Janos, Chihuahua State.

The battle of Janos has the true proportions of an epic. Thirty libertarians made hundreds of henchmen of the Porfirian dictatorship bite the dust in an embarrassing defeat, but during the action, the most sincere, selfless, and intelligent member of the Mexican Liberal Party lost his life.

The battle unfolded during the darkness of the night. Our thirty brothers, carrying the Red Flag—the insignia of the dispossessed of the world—threw themselves with courage against the town that was strongly garrisoned by the assassins of Capital and Authority. They were resolved to take the village or lose their lives in the attempt. The enemy's very first shots caused Praxedis to fall, mortally injured, never to rise again. A bullet had penetrated the right ear of the martyr, destroying the cerebral mass—that mass that had given off such intense light, making visible to the humble the path toward emancipation. And it must have been the hand of a dispossessed man—one of those who he wished to redeem—who fired the projectile that ended the life of the libertarian!

The combat lasted throughout the night. The enemy, convinced of its numerical supremacy, did not wish to surrender, hoping that it would forcibly crush the handful of the bold. The shots were fired at point-blank range, and combat proceeded hand-to-hand in the town's streets. The enemy attacked fiercely, as though it were assured of victory, while our own repelled such aggression with courage, knowing that they, being inferior in number, had to make marvels of courage and audacity.

The fight lasted throughout the night of December 30, until the approach of dawn, when the enemy fled, terrified, for Casas Grandes, leaving the countryside in the control of our brothers and a heap of corpses in the streets of Janos. The sun on December 31 shed light on the scene of tragedy, where two of our own lay: Praxedis and Chacón.[1]

Praxedis was simply a man, but a man in the true meaning of the word: not the atavistic, egotistical, calculating, evil mass-man, but rather the man freed of all types of prejudices, a man with an open intelligence who launched himself into the struggle without love for glory, love for money, or sentimentality. He went to the Revolution convinced of its merit. "I have no enthusiasm," he would tell me; "what I have is conviction."

Onlookers might imagine that Praxedis was a nervous and exalted man, affected by the spur of excitability. But no: Praxedis was a calm man who was extremely modest, both in theory and in practice. Being the enemy of silly vanity, he dressed very poorly. He did not drink wine like many frauds who boast of being abstinent: "I do not need it," he would say when he was offered a glass, and indeed, his calm temperament did not need alcohol.

Praxedis was heir to a rich fortune that he repudiated: "I have no heart for exploiting my fellow humans," he said. So he put himself to work shoulder-to-shoulder with his own farmhands, suffering their fatigue, participating in their pains, sharing their poverty. He was a child then, but he did not shirk before the very hard future that awaited him as a wage-slave. He worked for years in Mexico as a farmhand on the *haciendas*, as a stable boy in the rich houses of the cities, as a carpenter where he was given that sort of work, and as a mechanic in the railway workshops. At last

1   Who Chacón exactly was is unknown; presumably, he was a PLM militant serving with Praxedis who died during the battle of Janos.

he came to the United States, avid to learn about and see this civilization that is discussed so much in foreign countries, but like all
intelligent men, he was disappointed at the supposed grandeur of
this country of the dollar, of its intellectual insignificance, and of
its most stupid patriotism.

Here, in the land of the "free," in this home of the "brave,"
he suffered all the assaults, savage treatments, and humiliations to
which the Mexican worker is subjected by the bosses and the North
Americans who, in general, believe themselves to be superior to
us Mexicans, because we are Indians and mestizos of Spanish and
Indigenous blood. In Louisiana, a boss for whom he had worked
a few weeks was going to kill him for the "crime" of requesting
the payment of his wages.

Praxedis worked in wood-cutting in Texas, in the coal mines,
on the railways, on the wharfs of the ports. A true libertarian proletarian, he had a special aptitude for carrying out all types of
manual labor. That was how that large heart warmed up: through
misfortune. He was born in a rich crib and could have died in a
rich bed, but he was not one of those men who can calmly eat when
his neighbor is hungry.

Praxedis was, then, a proletarian, and due to his ideals and
acts, an anarchist. Wherever he traveled, he preached respect and
mutual aid as the strongest basis on which the social structure
of the future should rest. He spoke to the workers of the rights
that aid all human beings to live—and to live means to have an
assured home and food, and to enjoy, furthermore, all the advantages offered by modern civilization, given that this civilization is
nothing more than the joint efforts of thousands of generations
of workers, sages, and artists. As such, no one has the right to
appropriate these advantages for himself, leaving the rest in poverty and destitution.

Praxedis was very well known by the Mexican workers who
reside in the Southern States of this country, and the news of his
death caused great consternation in the humble homes of our
brothers living in misfortune and poverty. Each one of them had
a memory of the martyr. The women recalled how the apostle of

the modern ideas brandished the axe to help them split the wood with which to cook their poor foods—this, after having spent the entire day enclosed in the depths of a mine or having suffered the sun's rays working on the railways for twelve hours, or having worn himself out cutting down trees on the edge of the Mississippi. And the families, convening at night, heard the friendly and knowledgeable talk of this unique man who never walked alone. In his modest backpack he carried books, pamphlets, and revolutionary newspapers that he would read to the humble ones. The workers and their families remembered all of this upon learning that Praxedis G. Guerrero had died. No longer would the friend, the brother, and the teacher stay in those honest homes ...

And what will the son of the people have gained, he who upholds the capitalist system by having cut short the fertile life of the martyr?

Oh, soldiers who serve in the ranks of the State: each time that your rifle kills a revolutionary, you add yet another link to your chain! Return to reason, soldiers of Authority; you are poor, and your families are poor, so why do you kill those who would sacrifice everything to see all human beings free and happy?

Soldiers, turn the muzzles of your rifles against your chiefs and join the ranks of the rebels of the Red Flag, who struggle with the cry of Land and Freedom! Do not kill any more of the best of your brothers.

And you workers, think on the exemplary life of Praxedis G. Guerrero. See his face: it is a farmhand's shirt that he wears, and the attitude in which we see him now is the same he displayed when he had some sheets of paper in front of him onto which he generously poured his exquisite thoughts.

Praxedis G. Guerrero was the first Mexican anarchist who irrigated with his blood the virgin soil of Mexico, and the cry of "Land and Freedom" that he launched in an obscure village of Chihuahua State is now the cry that is heard from one side of the beautiful land of the Aztecs to the other.

Brother, your sacrifice was not in vain. When your drops of blood fell to the ground, they inspired thousands of heroes who will continue your work toward the goal of economic, political, and social freedom for the Mexican people.

Regeneración no. 70 (fourth edition), 30 December 1911

A Letter from Ricardo Flores Magón

Federal Penitentiary, Leavenworth, Kansas, July 23, 1922
To Nicolás T. Bernal, Mexico City

My beloved Nicolás:

The idea of this editorial group—to make known the incomparable works of Praxedis—is extremely brilliant.[1] Those works are not very well known, though they were published during a time when *Regeneración* had a print run of more than twenty thousand, if I do not recall incorrectly. It is unfortunate, however, that there is not a comrade there who had had the fortune of personally knowing our unsung Praxedis. If there were some such person, he could inform the slave, for whom the hero suffered and died, about the life of this exceptional man—poet, philosopher, and revolutionary—who shed such intense and pure light during his ephemeral existence. When I say exceptional, I do not refer solely to his literary labor that by itself speaks with exquisite eloquence to the marvelous character of Praxedis's brain, but also to his behavior as a man of principles, as a sincere apostle of the anarchist ideal, considering that, if anyone has lived within the Ideal and struggled in conformity with it, it was Praxedis, the landowner-farmhand, the capitalist-worker. Son of a powerful landowning family of the León District in Guanajuato State, the child Praxedis had his delicate

---

1   Magón is referring to the group comprised of Bernal, Librado Rivera, and Diego Abad de Santillán, who edited and published the volume on which this translation is based.

flesh wrapped in silk and brocades from the beginning of life. In this case, the poetic tradition regarding the extremely humble origin of the redeemers of the people was broken. Praxedis was not born in a manger; he was born rich and amidst wealth. He entered life to live the idle existence of the powerful, as immense were the lands that were his to inherit, and immense was the number of slaves that had to sweat and suffer for him. Everything indicated that the child Praxedis would be raised and live as a bourgeois, but here enters the extraordinary aspect of the case: the child Praxedis entered life with an exceptional sensitivity, and with an exceptional brain, too. He could understand that those farmhands who squandered their lives stooped over the bitter furrow, poor in intellectual light and material wealth, orphans of all rights and on whose scrawny shoulders rest all of society's weight, were his brothers—men whose only crime to merit the pitiful life of the beast of burden was the whim of a Fortune that did not want them to be born, like him, among silk and brocades, and the child's heart wept blood …

The child grew, and being a youth, he studied. He wanted to know; he wanted to investigate. In the presence of the Universe and in the stream of life his restless spirit asked, "Why? For what? From where? To where?" And as religion gave him no response that would satisfy his reason, he asked Science, and this, being always friendly, opened the dense curtains of the faith with which superstition limits the horizon of human knowledge, allowing him to glimpse the mysteries of the Cosmos and of Life … Then he understood that it was not Fortune that was responsible for the iniquity that was unfolding before his eyes, but rather social injustice, and against this injustice that reduces the human being to a beast of burden, his conscience rebelled, and he became a revolutionary. It was in this way that, upon the death of his father and when he was about to inherit formidable wealth, that he renounced his right to this and launched himself at the world to gain his bread with the sweat of his brow... Is this not extraordinary? There is an abundance of men of talent and geniuses—and Praxedis was a genius. But what is not in abundance is that generosity and constancy in the Ideal that make Praxedis G. Guerrero a sublime figure in the revolutionary history of the world, one whom we survivors love, just as we love that other giant of character known as Peter Kropotkin.

A revolutionary of action, he took an active part in the insurrectional movements of September 1906, June 1908, and November 1910 against the despotism of Porfirio Díaz, and at the front of a handful of brave ones he lost his invaluable life, at the young age of twenty-eight, in Janos, Chihuahua State, during the night of December 30, 1910, fighting for Land and Freedom. Words fail to relate the exemplary life of this distinguished revolutionary, whose strong relief could only be represented in marble or bronze. His life was short, but extremely fertile, and his death was a real loss for the cause of human emancipation. If he had not died, perhaps there would no longer be chains; if he had not died, perhaps man would have stopped exploiting and oppressing man. Who can know? His emancipatory work included the oppressed throughout the world, convinced as he was that evil was not exclusively a Mexican but rather a global issue, and that humanity suffers throughout the vast expanse of the planet, wherever there is someone who says, "This is mine!" or wherever there is someone who cries, "Obey!"

My congratulations to the beloved comrades who make up the editorial group, including you, my good and beloved Nicolás, for the happy idea of publishing the work of our unforgettable Praxedis.

With a strong embrace, your brother who loves you bids you farewell.

The Apostle

Journeying through the fields, traversing roads, advancing through the hawthorns and stones, and with his mouth dried by devastating thirst goes the Revolutionary Delegate on his catechist enterprise, below the sun that appears to avenge itself against his audacity by beaming down onto him its darts of fire. But the Delegate does not stop; he does not want to lose even one minute. From some hovel or another emerge sickly dogs to persecute him, being as hostile to him as the miserable residents of the hovels, who laugh stupidly at the passage of the apostle of the good news.

The Delegate advances; he wishes to reach that group of small friendly houses that give off light in the hillside of the high mountain, where he has been told comrades exist. The heat of the sun makes the journey intolerable; hunger and thirst debilitate him as much as the fatiguing march, but in his lucid mind the idea is conserved freshly and clearly like the water of the mountain, being as beautiful as the flower that cannot be touched by the threat of the tyrant. Such is the idea: it is immune to oppression.

The Delegate marches and marches. The barren fields oppress his heart. How many families would live in abundance if these lands were not in the hands of a few ambitious men! The Delegate continues his journey; a snake sounds its rattle beneath some dusty brush; the crickets fill the warm air with strident rumors; a cow lows in the distance.

At last the Delegate arrives at the hamlet, where he has been told there are comrades. Alarmed, the dogs bark at him. Through the doors of the homes peer indifferent faces. Below a vestibule there is a group of men and women. The apostle approaches them; the men frown; the women regard him with distrust.

"Good afternoon, comrades," says the Delegate.

Those in the group look at each other. No one responds to the greeting. The apostle does not give up, but repeats:

"Comrades, I come to give you good news: the Revolution has broken out."

No one responds; no one unlocks his lips; instead, they once again look at each other, their eyes trying to escape their orbits.

"Comrades," the propagandist continues, "tyranny is tottering; energetic men have wielded arms to bring it down, and we only await that all without exception assist those who struggle for freedom and justice in whatever manner."

The women yawn; the men scratch their heads; a hen passes through the group, persecuted by a rooster.

"Comrades," continues the indefatigable propagandist of the good news, "freedom requires sacrifices; your life is difficult; you have no satisfactions; the future of your children is uncertain. Why do you express indifference in the face of the selflessness of those who have launched themselves into the struggle to conquer your happiness, to make you free, so that your little children will be happier than you? Help; help in any way you can. Dedicate a part of your wages to fomenting the Revolution, or take up arms if you prefer: but do something for the cause. At least propagate the ideals of the grand insurrection."

The Delegate then paused. An eagle passed swaying in the clean air, as though it was the symbol of the thought of that man who, walking among human swine, preserved himself very tall, very pure, and very white.

The buzzing flies entered and exited the mouth of an old man who was asleep. The men, visibly annoyed, filed out one by one; all the women had already left. In the end only the Delegate remained in the presence of the old man who slept through his drunkenness and a dog who launched furious bites at the flies that sucked on his mange. Not a cent had emerged from those squalid pockets, nor did they offer a drop of water to that extremely firm man who, casting a compassionate look at that lair of egotism and stupidity, traveled to another little house. Passing in front of a tavern, he could see those miserable ones with whom he had spoken finishing glasses of wine, giving to the bourgeoisie what they did not wish to give to the Revolution, riveting their chains, and condemning their little children to slavery and shame due to their indifference and egoism.

The news of the arrival of the apostle had now spread through the whole village and, as the residents had been warned, they closed the doors of their homes upon the approach of the Delegate. Meanwhile a man, who according to his appearance should be a worker, arrived panting at the doors of a police station.

"Sir," said the man to the chief of the henchmen, "how much will you give us to hand over a revolutionary?"

"Twenty *reales*," said the thug.

The deal was closed; Judas had lowered the price. Moments later a man, bound hand and foot, was taken to the jail. Shoved, he fell, and after kicking him, the executioners picked him up, guffawing like drunken slaves. Some men took pleasure in throwing handfuls of dirt at the eyes of the martyr, who was none other than the apostle who had journeyed through the fields, traversed roads, advanced through hawthorns and stones, with his mouth dried by devastating thirst, but carrying in his lucid mind the idea of the regeneration of the human race by means of wellbeing and freedom.

Regeneración no. 19 (fourth edition), 7 January 1911

A Catastrophe

"I will not kill myself so that others live," said Pedro the miner in a clear voice when Juan, his co-worker, showed him a copy of the newspaper *Regeneración*, full of details of the revolutionary proletarian movement in Mexico. "I have a family," he continued, "and a fine beast I would be if I presented my belly to the bullets of the federal troops."

Juan received Pedro's observation without astonishment: that is how the majority speak. Some of them even tried to beat him when he told them that there are places where the farmhands had refused to acknowledge their masters and made themselves owners of the *haciendas*. A few days passed. Juan, after having bought a good carbine with an abundant supply of cartridges, traveled to the mountains where he knew rebels were. He was not interested in knowing which flag the revolutionaries flew, or which ideas they advanced. If they were his own, that is, of those who, flying the red flag, fight to make themselves strong so as to found a new society, in which each would be the master of herself and the executioner of none, very good—he would join them, thus adding with his person both to the number of fighters and to the numbers of brains involved in the great redemptory mission, which needs rifles and brains capable of illuminating other brains, as well as hearts capable of setting alight other hearts with the same fire. But even if those who prowled nearby were not his own, that didn't matter; he would join them in any case, as he considered it an obligation as a libertarian to intermix with his unconscious brothers to make them conscious by means of skillful conversations regarding the rights of the proletariat.

One day the wives of the miners crowded together at the entrance to a mine. A landslide had closed off one of the mine's galleries, trapping more than fifty workers. Pedro was among these and, like the others, had no hope of escaping death. In the darkness the poor laborer thought of his family: he would confront a horrifying agony, deprived of water and food, but in the end, after a few days, he would enter into the rest of death—what of his family? What would become of his wife or his little children? Then he thought angrily about the sterility of his sacrifice, and recognized too late that the anarchist Juan was right when, having shown him *Regeneración*, he had spoken to him enthusiastically about social revolution and the necessary class struggle, being indispensable so that man ceases to be the slave of man, so that all could bring food to their mouths, so that once and for all crime, prostitution, and poverty would come to an end. The poor miner then remembered that cruel sentence that he once had launched at the face of his friend Juan, as though it had been spit: "I will not kill myself so that others live."

While the buried-alive miner was thinking about working so that the bourgeois owners of the business lived, the women, weeping, writhing their arms, cried for their husbands, brothers, sons, and fathers to be returned to them. Groups of volunteers presented themselves to the business manager, requesting that he allow them to do something to rescue those unfortunate human beings, who awaited, in the mine, a slow and horrible death from hunger and thirst. The rescue operation began, but how slowly it advanced! Moreover, was it assured that the miners would be found alive? Had all forgotten that the bourgeoisie, so as to share and divide greater profits, did not provide sufficient wood to support the galleries, and that the very gallery in which the catastrophe had taken place had been the worst-reinforced? Regardless, men of good will worked, taking turns, day and night.[1] The families of

---

1   Compare Kropotkin's discussion in *Mutual Aid*, chapter 8, of volunteer rescuers in Lifeboat Associations and among the miners of the Rhonda Valley in Wales who risked their lives to save their trapped comrades.

the victims, being impoverished, did not receive from the bourgeois owners of the mine even one handful of maize with which to make a few tortillas and a bit of *atole*,[2] despite the fact that their husbands, brothers, sons, and fathers were owed wages for several weeks' work now.

Forty-eight hours had passed since the catastrophe had taken place. Outside, the sun illuminated the desolation of the miner's families, while in the bowels of the earth, in the darkness, the horrible tragedy came to its final act. Crazed by thirst and possessed by savage desperation, the miners with the weakest minds beat their picks furiously against the hard rock for a few minutes—only to fall prostate soon thereafter, some of them never to arise again. Pedro thought … "How blessed would Juan be at this moment: free like everyone who has a weapon in his hands, he is; satisfied like everyone who has a grand idea and who fights for it, he is. He, Juan, would at such moments be fighting against the soldiers of Authority, Capital, and the Clergy, precisely against the executioners who, out of a desire to not reduce their profits, were responsible for my being buried alive." Then he felt fits of fury against the capitalists, who suck the blood of the poor; then he recalled Juan's talks, which he had always found so boring, but which he now recognized for all the value they had. He remembered how one day Juan, as he was rolling a cigarette, spoke to him of the astonishing number of victims that industry produces annually in all countries, exerting himself to show Pedro that more humans die due to derailments, shipwrecks, fires, collapsed mines, and an infinity of workplace accidents than in the bloodiest Revolution, to say nothing of the thousands upon thousands of people who die of anemia, excessive work, malnutrition, and illnesses contracted in the poor hygienic conditions of the homes of the poor and in the factories, workshops, foundries, mines, and other sites of exploitation. He, Pedro, also recalled the disregard with which he had listened to Juan that time, and with what brutality he had

2   This Nahuatl word refers to the traditional Mexican maize-based beverage.

rejected him when the propagandist had advised him that he send a contribution, however little it might be, to the Revolutionary Council that works for the economic, political, and social freedom of the working class. He recalled that he had told Juan, "I am not such a blockhead as to give away my money. Better to use it to get drunk!" And something like remorse tortured his heart, and in the anguish of the moment, with the lucidity that sometimes comes at critical times, he thought that it would have been preferable to have died defending his class than to suffer this dark, odious death in order to give life to the crooked bourgeoisie. He thought of Juan lying prone, dodging the shots of the henchmen of tyranny; he imagined him radiating with joy and enthusiasm, bearing in his fists the blessed insignia of the oppressed, the red flag, or magnificent and beautiful, with his hair floating in the air in the middle of combat, throwing dynamite bombs against the enemy's trenches, or he saw him in front of a group of brave ones, arriving at a *hacienda* and telling the farmhands: "Take it all and work it yourselves, like human beings and not beasts of burden!" And the poor Pedro desired that life of Juan's, which he now understood as being fertile; but it was too late now. Though he was still alive, he was dead to the world ...

Fifteen days have passed since the catastrophe in the mine. Disheartened, the rescuers abandoned the project. The relatives of the dead miners had to leave the countryside because they could not pay the rent for their homes. Some of their daughters, sisters, and even widows sold kisses in the taverns for a piece of bread... Pedro's oldest son found himself incarcerated for having taken a few floorboards from the firm's yard to provide a bit of heat for the little room in which his mother found herself lying ill as a result of the moral shock she had suffered. All the relatives had gone to the mining company's offices to request the wages in arrears of their lost ones, but they received not a cent. The owners calculated the amounts in the manner of the "Great Captain,"[3] and the dead came

---

3   An allusion to Gonzálo Fernández de Córdoba (1453–1515), the "Great Captain" under Ferdinand II (1452–1516) who infamously

out indebted, and the poor families had nothing to pay the rent for their little homes. One beautiful day—given that nature is indifferent to human misery—when the sun broke its rays in a nearby pond and the birds, free of masters, worked in their own interests seeking out insects for themselves and their little chicks—on this beautiful day, a representative of Authority, dressed all in black like a vulture, accompanied by armed police, went from little house to little house throwing all these poor people into the street in the name of the Law and for the benefit of Capital.

That is how Capital pays those who sacrifice themselves for it.

Regeneración no. 72 (fourth edition), 13 January 1912

invented an exorbitant list of expenses to be sent to the king following the Naples military campaign of 1506.